Called and Chosen

Ten Catholic Women Tell Their Stories of
Inv tation and Ordination

D1069904

Called and Chosen

Ten Catholic Women Tell Their Stories of Invitation and Ordination

Edited by Sheila Durkin Dierks

WomenWord Press

Wo nWord Press
  Alp ne A n
Bou er,C O

Called and Chosen: Ten Catholic Women Tell Their Stories
of Inv tation and Ordination

Cop i t © by   Wo nWord Press
All ri t s reser d.P b ished
Printed in the United States of America

Book e sig b   Vick McVey
Co r desig b   essica Ku rm bs

Permissions to inclde indiv du l pe ms and essa ha b en
g anted b heir au hors.

ISBN: 1   5 -6

For all the women who came before,
especially those called and not chosen.

All creation is basically the work of imagination. To recreate the church is a work of the imagination. The radical imagination of these women is an ever-deepening dream of how the love of Jesus will be acted out in our time. Dreaming, envisioning, these are the works of imagination. Inspiration, yearning, desire, just anger, impatience, search, flowering, birth, poetry, justice, anticipation, New Creation.

Sheila Dn k n Dierk
WomenEucharist

CONTENTS

INTRODUCTION

Mary E. Hunt

The Catholic community is in the midst of its own Me-Too movement. Prompted by the unjust exclusion of women from ordained ministry and the jurisdiction (decision-making it confers under the current Roman Catholic Church rules, Catholic women are finding ways to exercise the many ministries to which they feel called. This volume includes the stories of ten such women. Literally thousands more women are waiting to tell theirs. Whether or not readers agree with all of the choices they make, it is imperative to believe them. The work ahead is to create the conditions in which women can bring their talents, studies, training and commitment to the common good.

Like its secular counterpart, this Catholic #MeToo movement is the result of many men with power, especially clerics, rejecting women's ministry. It springs from the men not believing women, questioning women's veracity, authenticity, and right to name their own vocations. Such treatment is violent. It has silenced women

for decades, causing many of them to ignore or deny what they
know to be true. Some women have literally been driven crazy,
like saints of old, when they were thwarted from being themselves.

Men who oppress women in this way do it because they can.
Many do not understand the damage that sexism, as well as, racism
and homohatred, cause to women themselves. They do not grasp
the negative consequences for the whole Catholic community
when only half are eligible to serve. Or, perhaps they do not care.

That p riod of chn ch historyi s coming o a close. Women
are now eng g d in sacramental ministrya lb it not sanctioned
b ,nor do theys eek sanction from,t he ky iarchal institu ion.
Ju t as the secu ar M eToo mov ment will not b stop d,ne i-
ther will Catholic women remain silent anym ore. The need for
ministrydoe s not cease ju t b cau e women are ex lde d. To the
contrary,now women who discern and train for ministryi n forms
that do not mirror the clerical,c elib te,a ll male model will b
the ones who fulfill the needs.

The mov ment for women's ordination dates to the early
worlof St.J oan's Alliance,a centu y old women's rib t s g op
that raised the ordination issu amongot her concerns in the
9 .U S .c itizen MaryB .L yc h discussed it with En op an
women who tog ther sp rk d the mov ment. The Women's Ordination Conference (WOC) p oi ded p oneeringa nd distinb shed
leadershipa nd is now p rt of the m b ella g op Women's Ordination Worldwide (WOW). The Women-Chn ch mov ment has
encon ag d my iad forms of women's ministry.

The stories in this bolm ak clear that manyw omen g t
hints and b imp es of their own ministerial vc ations indep n-
dent of anyc onferences or mov ments. They epr t this as a
call,a deeps ense of what theya re meant to do with their liv s
that simb ydoe s not g a wayov r time. The main model most
of them had was p iestlym inistryi n the Roman Catholic male
mold. That theyp rsisted in something hat theyc ou d not
imab nea— woman p iest was as lik lya s a p eba nt mans— ay

something a bt the streng h of their coni ction.F eminist scholars in relig on,e sp ciallyR osemaryR adford Ru ther and Elis-
ab th Schä sler Fiorenza,p oi ded the intellectu l fonda tions
and the lang g to name women's many oc ations.

The women in this collection tell of seri ce,l itn g ,t eaching
p eaching a nd administration in terms that b ar a resemb ance
to the roles of ordained Catholic male p iests.B t most Catholic
women in ministry e k end and reshap those roles in less hierar-
chical,m ore eg litarian forms.I n each case chronicled here,t he
woman fond a creatie way t o ex rcise her ministry w ell b -
ynd t he bnda ries of an ex ldi ng c ommni ty t hat rejected her
b cau e of her g nder and thu missed entirely t he friu ts of her
ministry.H ap ly,ot her su h commni ties that ap eciate wom-
en ministers are emerg ng a nd women are ministering i n those
with dedication and v re .

Each woman in this volume has a unique story. Some join
groups like the Ecumenical Catholic Communion, Roman Catholic WomenPriests, or the Association of Roman Catholic Women
Priests. Even more women, many of whose stories remain to be
told, have created and/or joined house churches, especially wom-
en-church groups. Some have led social justice organizations,
taught, preached, shared sacraments, and written as the fulfillment
of ministerial vocations that are effective and useful far beyond
the ecclesial constraints. Still others have been ordained in Protestant churches raising the question of whether their bi-denomina-
tionalism, as it were, makes them Catholic ministers as well.

This collection shows that there is no sing e p th to ex rcis-
ing p iesthood or ministry. The mu tip icity i s p oof that women
are not b nt on rep icating a k iarchal model,b coming he new
clerics. That collectie refu al,w ith few ex ep ions,t o rep icate
the patriarchal model has been clear since the first Women's
Ordination Conference in R ather,m ost Catholic women
ministers are k en to b ing heir b st sele s,t heir most inclu ie

embraces, and the experience and preparation needed to exercise effective ministry without the trapping of clerical privilege.

Women priests are not deluded into thinking that there is an ontological difference between them as clerics and so-called lay people. In this sense, they become the new role models for men who wish to minister. They live out egalitarian theologies that ought to be but clearly are not obvious to institutional church leaders who purport to read the same Gospel.

It is important to note that virtually all of women's education and training for ministry is self-funded. Male candidates for ministry are showered with generous scholarships from their communities or dioceses, even paid to go to seminary. We have one deeply appreciated scholarship fund, the Louisville Murray Dunkin Scholarship For Women Discerning Priestly Ordination (http://www.womensordinationorg/programs/scholarship). By its very existence this fund encourages women to think for and about themselves as priestly people. More such financial support is needed especially for those who are younger, women of color, LGBTIQ, or otherwise marginalized.

Many women are still not welcome to study in some Catholic seminaries. Virtually no women receive the moral and spiritual support that surrounds any man who evidences the least inkling of interest in ordained ministry. These facts add up to an even more compelling case for the power of women's vocations to ministry against formidable odds. For women of color the odds increase exponentially. Imagine if men were subject to the same conditions. It is doubtful that there would be any priests at all.

All of this is happening while the Roman Catholic Church is imploding. Priest pedophilia and its cover-up, clerics engaging in *quid pro quo* sexual relationships with subordinates (à la Theodore McCarrick), and the still-to-be-told stories of male priests sexually abusing women form a constellation of issues that has eroded trust, confidence, and even interest in the institutional church.

The denial of women's right to test their priestly calls, the continued resistance to women deacons, the refusal to let lay women vote in church synods despite the fact that lay men can, and the shameful treatment of LGBTIQA people scandalize all but the most recalcitrant believers. The exodus from the institutional church has become a stampede for the doors, as even some of the most fervent adherents cannot stomach the moral bankruptcy. It is obvious why women are needed more than ever in ministry.

The iv rli ence with which the institu ional chn ch has cast women in ministrya side is in p rt an effort to distract attention from some men's criminal b haiv or. There is a strong ase to b made that ex ldi ng atholic women longa fter other Christian denominations saw the lit of ministerial eq lityw as a des-p rate reaction to somethingn ore.I t was the Roman Catholic Chn ch's panic at the ps sib lityof female p ofessional col-leag s seeing he work ng of the institu ional chn ch close p for fear that the women woli d b ow the whistle.I t work d nt il now,w hen g and jn ies,s þe na pw er,a nd ev n the Js tice Dep rtment are doing he joif or a .

The coincidence of women steþ ngf orward to ex rcise min-istrya t a time when the institu ional stru tn es and its p rsonnel are incap b e of meeting he needs of the commni tyi s p rhap p oiv dential. Yet well-intentioned women ma t refa e to clean p the horrific mess that patriarchal theology, clerical entitlement, eþ scoþ l dþ icity, and wholesale disreg rd for the Gosþ l hav wroht . The institu ional stru tn es are simþ ynot worth saiv ng safer more effectiv ones can b created.B ti the needs of p oþ e who hav a rit to ministrydo not g a way. Theya re the foca of and the measn e ag inst which ev rym inister is ex la ted.

Still,t here is somethingni q lyi mpr tant abti the fact that well trained,de eþ ys þ rita l,w idelye þ rienced women are ready,w illinga nd ab e to handle the cn rent p storal emerg ncy. Spr tingy ctim/sn iv or s,þ tinga n end to ab e,a nd creat-ingne w forms of chn ch will b the task of ordinary ime for the foreseeable future. All this is on top of the day to-day's spiritual needs of communities in which babies are born, people get sick and die, and in which regular celebration of the Eucharist is sustaining. Catholics need all the ministers we can get.

The women whose stories are gathered here are already ministering. They are developing new communities. They have a profound respect for the wide range of religious traditions and experiences that form the contemporary spiritual landscape. They bring their Catholic backgrounds to a 'catholic' context. They recognize the power of sacrament and solidarity in nurturing faith communities. They also realize that they minister to the whole community, not simply to those of their faith tradition.

Many of these women represent a long-standing sense of their own ministerial identity. Without making a virtue of necessity, their very rejection has spurred them to rethink the givens of patriarchal models of church and ministers, and to imagine very different ways of being ministers and priests, fresh titles, roles, and tasks that will build community, accomplish justice, and nurture the spirits of their members. This bodes well for all of us.

I hope that this collection is simply the first of many in which the moving authentic, sometimes complicated yet always faithful stories of women priests and ministers' lives will help readers reflect on their own. All Christians are called and chosen to embrace their baptismal promises and engage in ministry of Word and Sacrament as part of egalitarian, justice-making communities. Thanks to these ten women for offering their experiences as shining examples of what Catholic ministry look like in the twenty-first century.

CARITAS VERITAS
CALLED TO ORDINATION: SO, WHAT IF IT'S A GIRL?

Sheila Durkin Dierks

I grew up in a house before Television. Not just without TV, before TV. So what did we know? We three girls were undisturbed by cartoons, sit coms, children's shows. Like many families, we centered around our Catholic parish, which was our primary entertainment. We were immersed in the stories of the Church year. The flow of Advent to Christmas, Lent to Easter. The vivid stories of Annunciation to Resurrection were our stories.

My old er sister Ellen, e v n in early g ade school, ha d a ka ck for writing p lay . S he woli d u e a Bib e story a s the b sis, p in dialog , and assig r oles. We p on p rformances that u ed p op from the hos e, i ncldi ng he g een k tchen step tool on which Ellen, dr essed in a b throb , w ith a man's tie around he r forehead, w oli d þ ayJ ess , a nd ascend into heav n. On sister Frances, yu ng r, di d not g t dialog and often had to b a shepe rd. The y rdstickf rom the b sement was her staff. We woli d g ther pp rents and sit them on the liv ng oom cou h, and then they would muffle their laughter as we played out the lives of Jesus and Mary and their friends.

Part of this imaginative life was, for me, the funniest: My first vestment, a blue bath towel with my mother's monogram in a triangle-form in pink, a remnant of her trousseau. I have it still. It went with me to the ordination and was part of my ordination liturgy.

This was all part of the harmless imagination by which we discover our lives. And part of the truth-telling too. Children always do it.

I remember the moment: Crystalline. I recall the feeling of the air, the slant of light. There was a powerful presence. I knew, perfectly, what I was going to be when I grew up. I was six years old.

Could this be Veritas?

Excited, I told my mother.

Her response: You can't be a priest. Girls can't be priests, only boys can be priests.

❡

My *What I'm going to be when I grow up* moment was challenged, but not spoiled. AND it was the first time I knew that there were people who thought there were differences in what girls and boys can do.

So, I invite you to think for a moment of the slow or lightning fast dawning of your invitation to become that to which you are called.

Playing teacher? Boarding a plane and seeing the pilot, boarding the plane and seeing the stewardess? Building egg towers? Discovering the magic of your mom's lap or computer? Feeding people who had no dinner?

These experiences are not just child's play. How often the invitation is a pre-figuring. The ones that are simply whims fade in the child's imagination. The ones that need attention remain and reoccur. I call that, *insistence.* Graham Greene tells us that there

is alway a moment in childhood when the door op ns to let the
fu n e in (Greene ﬞ   .

That was mym oment. And that moment has liœ d in me eœ r
since. I have affinity for the like-me story of Samuel, Old Testament yng hild in the temþ e,a nd his inœ tation,a n ne þ cted
œi ce. An inœ tation,a þ ckni ng hat is reallyi rresistib e. The
same was tru of Maryt he Nazarene,a near-child in her g rden.
Those stories neœ r seemed strang to me.I nde rstood.S amu l
was immediately affirmed. He was in the inner sanctm ,þy i-
callya nd þ inœ tation. Marý s respns e was,“ How can this þ ?”
It woｈ d need to nf old for her.

What is it to þ tou hed ｻ he most p ofond m oment of
yn œ rys hort life and then haœ the liｧt fade and normalcy
retn n? I susp ct I tookof f myｾ th towel œ stment and went to
set the dinner tab e. Yet in that moment,l ife chang d.

Youㅁ re immersed in a ｨow ingnot of yn own mak ng.
Transformed and ｹ t same. You tell and are immediatelyœ m-
braced and encouraged, because you have fulfilled expectations.
Or yuㅁ re challeng d,þ cas e yｻha œ þ ok n with nde rstood
role and g nder models.N ot jㅁ t,“ Girls can’t,” þ p ofondl y,
“It is wrong o want it.” Can the Diœ ne Inœ ter onlyc all those
who have been declared fit and worthy by a manufactured human
model for g nder deœ lopﾊ ent?

And therein lies the neｫ stepof this jon ney. What Veritas is
there,i n this inœ tation?

Can it þ tru ? Can it þ of God,i f the inœ tation is eｫ ended
to a ｇ rl? And if so,how can it þ accomþ ished?

For those of us who experienced this—especially when
the people we loved, and the people who were Wisdom-Guid-
ance-Authority, denied the possibility of any such invitation—
we asked then, and continued to ask, can this be Veritas? Can
it be tested?

And so we dismiss,a nd do on times tab es,a nd memorize
œc ab ary,g on da tes,œ lnt eer,f all in loœ ,f all ou of loœ ,

9

graduate ...and yet the power of this foolishness persists. We do not talk about it. There is no path in high school for girls.

When I was in college, there was no invitation, no way the question of women being ordained was ever raised, though it lived in me. I was no longer a praying priest. I could not see my place in such a deliberately exclusive male world.

I spent the next forty years running a shelter for homeless families, being married, raising our children, I was teaching a liberated faith tradition in a progressive Catholic school, working at the Catholic Worker, planning liturgies for the parish, marching for jobs and housing, looking back now, I see this as the progression of development of the Caritas of priesthood. If I had been male, others would have noticed, but we all note that we are often blind to what we do not believe is possible ...what we have been taught with great certainty is not possible.

～

My Scripture writers became Joan Chittister, Rosemary Reuther, Miriam Therese Winter, Gerda Lerner, Morwood and Schillibeeck, Mary Hunt, Lavinia Byrne, Pheme Perkins, and a hundred others: The women theologians and historians who un-covered the ancient possibilities that women had been ordained in the distant past before it was forbidden, and those histories were suppressed. Gary Macy's, John Wijngaard's groundbreaking work told us of the re-discovered ordination rites for women as well as men. Rites that met all the conditions for major orders. I would wonder, How did they celebrate? What words did they use? And did they pray while they preached the bread down and shaped it into royal loaves and baked it?

I later realized that all this was my schooling, my diaconal work. Part of Priestly Preparation. Caritas, Veritas. It was service and learning in the presence of the Divine, in the midst of the human community, in suffering and joy, and loneliness. Between, I was diaper changing and stirring the "almost taller than I am" sompt ,ha v ng drinkw ith friends and family,gi ng o the moi es and on children's school for conferences and children's p rformances.M eanwhile on diocese in New Jerseyw as b coming more rep essiv ,a nd I and others were hai ng a slow awakening

Forb dden anm ore to u e inclu iv lang g ,de nied a role at the altar, a g opf women of myp rish,t welv of the wisest women I kow ,g thered in fear,a nd excitement,a nd b g n to plan for our first Eucharistic liturgy. Antonia Malone, one of the wisdom women of myl ife and on diocese,a p ofessor at a local ni v rsity,a well-edu ated and wittyC atholic woman who had b en in the g nder-trenches for decades, joined with me in writing our first liturgy. She, tall, elegant, a figure of perfect poise who had had manye ncout ers with the ep scop cy,s at with me and a dozen bok on litn g .I rememb r the ligt ,a nd the freshness of the air, and the sense of fear in me,a nd the an a of certaintyt hat emanated from Tonie.

What we had felt ic all,i ni tation,w e b g n to liv otu . We sat arond t he tab e in a familyr oom,w ith chairs set p amidst toy and the TV Gu de,a nd shared wisdom that b ogt the words of the Gosp ls into on liv s. Women with deg ees in theolog nd scrip n e,a s well as g ade school teachers and retired office workers, helped guide our conversations. And there was a loaf of warm b ead and a cpf god w ine (we alway insisted on god w ine). And so what we call WomenEu harist b g n.

We ep rimented with inclu iv lang g ,i n scrip n e,i n sacrament. We followed the Eu haristic stru tn e,b cau e that is on sacred home ep rience. We b g n to recogi ze in this sacred encout er the p in of the world,t he strg es of p op e, those who coh d hav little p ace in chn ch and world. We b g n to recogi ze the hop that the Jesu sacrament embdi ed. And this is Caritas. And this is joy.

We call it Eucharist, Greek for thanksgiving. That was what we experienced. We set the table, baked the bread, gathered and organized, but the words of consecration were said by all. We began to have interior affirmation of the Veritas, the truth of our lived experience.

There are other groups like us who emerged as the word spread, quietly, a phone call, an email, a cup of coffee, and we discovered celebrations in Minneapolis, Los Angeles, Lima, Peru, women religious who celebrated in Chicago, Milwaukee, Kankakee, Cincinnati. Each group had one or two women who had felt an invitation to ordination. Women quietly gathering in each other's homes, like the early Christian community, sharing the sacred, praying the words of Consecration, breaking and sharing and telling our stories around the Eucharistic table. Pressed on by the necessity. Veritas/Caritas.

When we knew where the groups were I decided a book was a way to gather the voices of women nationwide. In 1997, I finished writing WomenEucharist, a narrative study of thirty sacramental groups, using the testimonies of hundreds of women. This all led me not only to look forward, asking *Where are we imagining toward?*, but also to look back. How many women invited to priesthood are there?

I had a profound moment.

At a Call To Action conference in Milwaukee, a group of perhaps 40 were asked: Would any women who have felt a call to ordination please stand. Perhaps eight women, most of them over fifty, stood. Eight women. Eight women. Veritas. I was not alone. Here were other women who might remember in the slant of light and the feel of the air, a presence and an invitation.

That led me to ask, How is it that the Divine Inviter might call someone to priestly ministry and then not wish them ordained to serve the people in waiting? What happened in the first centuries of the Christian communities, after Jesus? What happened to all the women who were last at the Cross, first at the

Tomb; and their sisters,t he ones who lifted up he bread of the
Passover meal? Did God bypass them in celebration? How could
that b Veritas?

I fond a g eat g ft, The Ecm enical Catholic Commni on,a
Catholic sister to The Roman Catholic Chn ch,s haring n what is
know n as aps tolic su cession,i ndep ndent since Vatican I,t hat
ordains women and men. Theyor dain p op e called and dis-
cerned.M arried,s ing e,di or ced,g y,s traigt ,c alled. Accep ed
in discernment, I sat monthlyf or two y ars,w ith a committee
of wisdom folk from myf aith commni ty. Theyj on ney d with
me. Their ga l,on ga l,w as to test myc all. Tell s yn story,
theys aid. Tell s abtu yn life of serv ceof commni tyof
sacrament... What are yn falu ts? Tell s abtu lov . Tell s
what yub liev ,w hat yuknow ,w hat can es yuw onder...
What do you find sacred?

MEANWHILE,he re is what the Catholic Chn ch of the Res-
n rection say on their web ite to yngm en abtu Call:

"The first sign that Jesus may well be calling you . . . is a
strongf eelingde epw ithin yuI t is there that the oi ce of Jesu
will reach,s tirringyut o listen more deep ya nd to discov r his
lov ngv ill for yui n his Chn ch.

Youm ay alreadyha v had su h feeling in the p st.P erhap
at p imarys chool yus ed to dress pa s a p iest and p aya t say-
ingM ass! Perhap yup hed the idea to one side,e mb rrassed,
ank on and rather afraid."

(resn rectionc oz a/main/sacraments/7 2)

∾

I went to seminary for a Masters in Theology. I was
ordained a Deacon in March 2008, served in preaching and
at the altar, and was ordained a priest on September 9, 2009.
Sixty-six years old. Sixty years since I first felt the invitation
in a bungalow living room,I N SUBURBAN CINCINNATI,
dressed in mym other's b th towel.

If you came to be part of the sacramental community of Light of Christ, and now at The Community in Discernment, here's what you might experience: Bread, a loaf, gluten-free, so that all are welcome. There will be good red wine. Inclusive language in scripture and sacrament. God is not He only, but She, Spirit, Divine Imagination, Creator, Birther, Friend and Amazement. God is Whisper and Possibility.

You will be welcomed to sit in the circle of which the priest a member. You will hear the scriptures read, listen to the Spirited wisdom of the presider, and also the sisters and brothers to your right and left as you weave a response that comes from your heart. You will be invited to speak of your worries and joys in the prayers of the people. You will be invited to participate in the words of the Eucharistic Prayer in which we, all together, bless the bread and wine and invite the Holy to reveal herself, himself, as center and meal, hope and salvation. You will find that, just as around our dinner tables, all are welcome. Radical Inclusion. There is no litmus test of worthiness. The sacred food is there for all of us. Unquestioned hospitality.

And then, together with everyone, you will share the holy meal. No questions. Eucharist, Thanksgiving belong to us all. Eucharist, yes. But also Reconciliation. Funerals, yes. Weddings, yes, where two people, woman and man, man and man, woman and woman, promise their love, discerning and affirming. .

Can women be ordained? Yes, careful scholarship tells us they were. The discovered rituals say they were. The archeology supports this information. Hundreds and hundreds of women, especially in the near East and Greece, whose burial stones identify them as ordained.

The documents unearthed in the library at Notre Dame in Paris, the ordination sacramentaries in the cathedral libraries of York and Exeter, of St Bleivnsa— all together there are so far six sacramentaries and nine pontificals that contain ordination liturgies for women as well as men!

Women who, for generations, set the table and baked the bread, and said the blessing? The ritual experience at altar and in living rooms where we are led to rediscover the sacred meal, with all its meanings and hopes and humility and blessing, with all its EUCHARIST, is the growing, regrowing CARITAS of communities, the VERITAS that women have long known, the blessing and breaking of communities into the Body and Blood of Jesus.

Amen and Allelu a

~

Women's Ordination in the EarlyC hn ch

This b ief rei ew of the earlyhi storyof women's ordination is b sed on research comp led b The Wigg ards Institu e for Catholic Research,a nd can b fond on t heir web ites:

<wwww omenp iestsor g and <wwww omendeaconsor g

During the first millennium tens of thousands of women serv d as ordained deacons,e sp ciallyi n the Greek sp ak ng p rt of the Catholic Chn ch. Their diaconal ordination inclde d:

1O rdination in front of the altar

2P b ic election throg t he Div ne Grace formu a

3L ay ngon of hands with the invc ation of the HolyS p rit

4 A second ordination p ay r with renewed lay ngon of hands and the callingdow n of the Sp rit

5R eceiv ng he distinctiv diaconate stole

6R eceiv ng he pw er to hold the chalice with the consecrated bdya nd b ood.

The Model Ordination Prayer

Of con se,t he orig nal "model p ay r," handed on in oral tradition,w ou d soon hav b en committed to p p s . The same hap ned to the oral tradition of Jesu ' deeds and words. We may safelya ssm e that short,w ritten litn g cal tek s ek sted bt he beginning of the second century. The first texts were, perhaps, written in GreekS oon a Latin v rsion woli d hav b en noted down.

Jս t as with the On Father and the Eս haristic Consecration p ay r,once a tex was written down it tended to "freeze", to b come a more rig d formli a that woli d not chang ov r time.I t migt b eℊ nded on,ob oս ly,ħ the orig nal oldest formli a woli d b p ssed on from one written tex to another.

From liturgical texts of later centuries that have been pre-served, we can identify the formula of the model ordination prayer. What is more, it shows that the same prayer was used both for priests, male deacons and female deacons. All that needed to be done was adapt certain element to the particular ordination.

Our sources are six sacramentaries and nine pontificals. They all p eserv the main ordination p ay r,a s well as later ex en-sions. The words of this p ay r are as follows:
"Hear,o L ord,on petition and send down on this ℊ maidser-ℊ nt the Sp rit of ℊ ordination so that,s ince ℊtha v con-ferred on her your heavenly office, she may obtain favour with ℊ majestℊ nd mayℊ esent to others the ex mþ e of a god life. Throħ ..."

What is the flu l meaningℊf this tex ? We can looℊ t the p ay r þr ase þr ase,a nd b eaℊ t down as follows into the Latin (first line), then the English translation (second line), and finally a brief commentary.
1 *Exaudi, Domine, preces nesters*
"Hear,O Lord,on pray rs .."
Candidates for the eþ scoℊ cy,p iesthood or diaconate were selected þ icly. The ordination was condu ted in the middle of the litn ℊ nd in ѵ ew of the whole cong eℊ tion.B oth clerℊ and p oþ e spr t the ordainingþ shop
2 *et super hunc (hanc) famulum tuum (famulam tuam)*
"and onto this [man/woman] ℊ manserℊ nt/maidserℊ nt .."
These words imþ ℊt hat the b shopѵ as imps ingħi s hand on the head of the candidate [male=famli m ; - female=famli am].

3 *spiritus*
"the Sp rit .."
The classical formla a of ordination reщ res the callingdow n of
the HolyS p rit on the candidate.
4 *tuae benedictionis emitte*
"of yn ordination send down .."
Benedictio can also mean "b essing Bu in the contek of
b essingb shop ,p iests or deacons it means what we call "ordination" today.I n other words: the ancient term for ordination was
"b essing
5 *ut caelesti munere ditatus (ditata)*
so that since yuha v conferred on him (her) yn heav nly
office
"enriched by your heavenly office . . ."
The latin word "munus" stands for a task, a job, a duty, an office.
Classical writers а e it for the taskof a soldier,t he ps t of am-
bassador, the ministry of an official. Here it clearly refers to the
diaconate ministryc onferred on the candidate.
6 *et tuae gratiam possit majestatis acquirer*
"he (she) maybt h ob ain favn with yn majesty.."
Officials who perform their task well will find favor with the
p rson who api nted them to the task
7 *et bene vivendi aliis exemplum praebere.*
"and p esent to others the ex mþ e of a god l ife."
The deacon's task s a þ ic fnc tion.I t carries with it the respns ib lityof g iv nga god e x mþ e to the commni ty.

What are our SOURCES?

Selected Sacramentaries

The Hadrianum Sacramentary preserves the model ordination
prayer quoted on the previous page. It is considered by scholars
to have been derived from the (now lost) Proto Gregorian Sacramentary, which was assembled by Pope Gregory I (590-604) and
which included ordination prayers. One of these is the Hadrianum.

Selected Pontificals

• C. 9 reserv s the cap b lity of b ing ordained to men only a nd therefore ex lde s women from the p iesthood and the sacramental diaconate.I t shou d howev r b noted that the magisterim has not p this p ecise q stion in the area of div ne law (c.9 . This retu ns the b sic q stion to the theolog cal "mag sterim " from which no leg slation,of any k nd whatev r, ex lde s women,b from which she is consp cou ly a b ent, that is,e x lde d in fact.

• Women do not,m oreov r,e njoy he fu l rigt s and duties of the laity since the role of reader and acoly e that are op n to lay p op e (c.9 are ep icitly eserv d to men.

Giv n that there are thou ands of women,t hrogou the world,r eady o tak on "ministerial" task far ex eeding hose p ovi ded for readers and acoly es,t hat they a re school,p ison and hosp tal chap ains,r espns ib e for p rishes,e tc,t hat they teach p iests,w ho are sometimes nde r their au hority,i t mu t b ag eed that these notoriou discriminatory c anons are p ob b y not there b hance.

IF I WAS MALE AND SINGLE

Denise Donato

If only the eight-year-old girl, whose heart was broken when she was told she couldn't be an altar boy, could have known about the journey of the sixty-year-old woman who would be the first woman consecrated as a bishop in the Ecumenical Catholic Communion. I suppose John White knew what he was talking about twenty-five years ago when he told me that Jesus was holding a staff, which he was giving to give to me when the time was right. "It will be your choice whether to take it or not. You still have gifts to develop," he said. "I know that because the staff is intricately carved to a certain point. But someday Jesus will offer that staff to you and you will need to decide whether to accept it or not. You need to know," he continued, "that I am not a Christian. I do not usually experience Jesus walking in with someone. Master Teachers are dressed in blue, there are various Master Teachers here, and the one holding the staff for you is Jesus."

Growing up in a traditional Italian Catholic family the little girl could never have imagined any of this! All I knew at the tender age of eight was that deep within my heart there was a desire, a longing to be closer to the altar. I had watched the altar boys ever rymore with yearning. I knew when it was time to bring the bowl of water for the priest to wash his hands, when to ring the bells, and the most important of jobs, how to hold the gold plate under the chin of each person, just in case the precious Body of Christ slipped from the communicant's tongue. I was sure I knew it better than many of boys who sat in the chairs on the altar yawning every Sunday. My mother told me that if I wanted to be an altar boy I would need to ask the priest. When I finally got the nerve, I was shot down in the blink of an eye—my spirit was crushed!

However, the longing in my heart only grew stronger! Once I got my driver's license I started to attend the 6:30 a.m. Wednesday morning Mass in the basement of the rectory. It was me, the priest, and five or six businessmen every Wednesday morning, in a dank dark basement, with buckets catching the water dripping from the waterlines, but I loved it! We all stood around the altar at the Eucharist and lifted our hands as Fr. Kreckle lifted the bread and wine and my spirit soared. I couldn't understand why one of the boys in my fellowship group were talking about going into the priesthood—what a wonderful opportunity this was! When I voiced my query, they looked at me like I was crazy. "But, just think about leading Mass, helping people on their faith journey. You're missing out on such a great opportunity." "If it's so great why don't you become a nun?" they said. "I don't want to be a nun!!" I vehemently responded, but I stopped short of uttering what was deepest within me. I couldn't admit, even to myself, that I longed to be a priest. It seemed blasphemous. My Catholicism had led me to believe that God doesn't call women to the priesthood. Period. End of the story. As such, my prayer often ended with the sentence: "If I was male and since I would know what this means." I knew that God was calling me to something more, something deeper, something that felt like a vocation, but I clearly did not feel a calling to become a nun, and as a woman this was the only option.

I carried this yearning in my heart into adulthood: "If I was male and single...". I could not complete the sentence. I wasn't male and having met and married my high school sweetheart I was no longer single, and there were no roads that led down that path for me. Others saw it in me as well: "Perhaps you should become Episcopalian or Methodist," they would say, but I didn't feel called to leave the Roman Catholic Church. This calling within my heart was deep but my faith tradition was equally deep for me. As an Italian Catholic woman, it seemed like Catholicism was a part of my DNA. "I don't feel called to leave my faith," I said.

I encountered this calling yet again in the 90s when I made the nineteenth annotation of the Spiritual Exercises of St Ignatius retreat through the Sisters of Mercy in Rochester, N.Y. It was the second week of this thirty week retreat, and I was praying on Moses and the burning bush. "Lord, I feel your calling me a deeper calling than I could have even imagined. If I was male and single I would know that I'm called to the priesthood." As I wrote these words in my journal it was the first time I had ever dared to finish the sentence. My shirt was wet from the rivulets of tears streaming down my cheeks. I had said it! But I paused. It felt sacrilegious to let the declaration stand on its own, so I continued. "But I'm not—so I must be mistaken." The longing in my heart was greater than ever, but the pain of finally admitting it, and realizing there was no path leading to its fulfillment, was even greater. Oddly, instead of questioning the church, I began to question myself. If God doesn't call women to the priesthood, I must be really full of myself to believe God was calling me. I spent the next eight years in this painful process of beginning to acknowledge the call, only to disparage myself for believing it. As Teresa of Avila indicates in her book *Interior Castle*, we expect that the closer we get to God the holier we will feel. However, quite the opposite is true. When we come into the intensity of the Divine Light we see our shadow side more clearly. Rather than feeling holy, the predominant feeling is one of unworthiness. It is true that a feeling of unworthiness often accompanies a true calling but the places I went were dyed deep and dark. My calling was tainted with the misconception that because women are not allowed to be ordained in the Roman Catholic Church, God must not call women, so I must be full of the deadly sin of pride!

All of this began to change when I had another prayer experience. In my prayer I experienced Jesus giving me a gift. My heart leapt as he handed it to me, beautifully wrapped with a big red bow on top. However, as Jesus handed me this gift I suddenly began to sob as I immediately knew that the gift in the box was ordination, and as long as I remained in the Roman Catholic Church I would never be able to open the box... unless trying it on for size to see how it looked on me! This prayer experience broke my heart, as I immediately knew I wasn't crazy—God was indeed calling me to ordination. But what was I to do? I still did not feel that God was calling me to leave Catholicism. I suddenly realized that my continual questioning of this call, and my merciless denigration of myself in the process, had served a purpose. As painful as it was, it had held back the greater pain of realizing that the deep call of my heart, and the Church that was seemingly so integral to my identity, were at odds with each other. And suddenly there was no solace in either one! This pain was deep.

Was this gift a burden I was called to bear, my cross for life, a divine exercise in frustration? While I wasn't sure where it was going or going, over the weeks that followed, as I continued to process this prayer experience, there were some things that became crystal clear. God was not bound by the rules of any institution, not even the Roman Catholic Church. I knew this—of course I like with— there had been times over the past eight years when the cannons that had been drilled into me, seemingly from birth, caused me to question myself. Besides that what do I know? The Church has been established for millennia, and it has been run by men who had far more education than I did. In addition, I had assumed, and had been taught, that the Catholic Church had been instituted, or at least intended by Jesus, as his continuing ministry in our world.

Yet even in the midst of the pain there were times when I had this fleeting sense that it would come to fruition. And as crazy as it seemed to me, I found some peace in that.

In I felt that I had an answer to my prayer. I was hired as the Family Minister at Corpus Christi Church, a very progressive church that many considered to be the last stop on the Roman Catholic Train. This was a church that was alive! They walked the talk of social justice and carried that social justice not only to those in need outside the church, but within the church as well. Everyone was invited to the Eucharistic Table; they believed that the sacraments should be open to all people and consequently married same sex couples; they believed in the ordination of women, and although they could not ordain women they had women in positions of leadership on the altar as well as ministering within the community. I knew that while I may never be ordained in the Roman Catholic Church, I could be actively involved in ministry at Corpus Christi.

Then in June of I was contacted by the religion editor of our local newspaper. He was doing an article on the ordination of women through the lens of various religious traditions, and he wanted to interview me on my call and what my experience was like as a Roman Catholic woman. After the interview I was scheduled to do a noon Communion Service, and he and his photographer tagged along. The story was scheduled to appear in the religion section of the Friday newspaper in a couple of weeks. Imagine my surprise when I pulled my newspaper out of the tube on Father's Day, flopped it open, and saw a big picture of me at the altar holding the Eucharist, front and center on the front page! "Oh my," I said, "I guess the Holy Spirit wants this to be front page news." It was the proverbial straw that broke the camel's back. There were conservative watchdogs in Rochester who made it their business to keep the Vatican informed of anything and everything that happened at Corpus Christi Church. I was sure a copy of this article would be expedited to Rome.

A few short weeks later that was confirmed. August 1998 Fr. Jim Callan, our pastor, was called into the Diocesan office and advised that the bishop had received a letter from then Cardinal Ratzinger, calling for his removal as pastor of Corpus Christi as a result of three things. These were: 1) everyone was invited to receive Eucharist, 2) we were marrying same-sex couples and 3) women were in leadership positions both at the altar and in every aspect of ministry. I'm sure the Vatican assumed that if they removed the priest, the community would fall back in line. They were wrong. The community organized. There were people who came that night to a meeting at church, and they were radicalized. They held rallies, prayer marches, wrote letters, organized an education series and worked with the media. Over the course of the next four months, Mary Ramerman, our associate pastor, was fired, they brought in a new priest whose job was to bring the community back in line with Rome, and on December 13 they fired six of us. Corpus Christi Church went from being a vibrant community that had few worshipers every Sunday, to having people in the pews. But from the ashes of Corpus Christi, Spiritus Christi was born, and with it brand new possibilities.

As this community formed we found a new joy that, after the despair of the dismantling of Corpus Christi, the assault of being told we had excommunicated ourselves from the Roman Catholic Church, and the deep pain of seeing something so beautiful reduced to ashes, had seemed beyond our ability to comprehend.

We fond a n ni mag ned freedom from the narrowness of the hi-
erarchyof the Roman Chn ch. We were celeb atingv ithou fear
of b ings hu down,y t we realized there was one asp ct of on
p actice that we were not fu lyl iv ng women were in leadership
roles b were not y t eq l b cas e theyw ere not y t ordained.

Realizing hat on Catholicism and its sacraments were near
and dear to on hearts,a ctu lizing his was not a simp e matter.
But slowly our journey began to find a path to ordination for
women that honored who we were at on core. MaryR amerman,
who was now the p stor of Sp ritu Christi Chn ch,l earned of
a Bishop n California who had ju t ordained a woman,a nd she
sogt him ou . While BishopP eter Hickn an was not Roman
Catholic,he was ordained iv a a strain of Catholicism that had
b ok n with the Roman Catholic Chn ch in the late 8 as a
resu t of the introdu tion of the concep of p p l infallib litya t
the First Vatican Conc il. The g opof b shop who b ok with
Rome referred to themselv s as Old Catholic,a s theyw ere relat-
ing hemselv s to the institu ion of the Chn ch that was p e-Vati-
can Conc il I. Theyha v a v lid line of aps tolic su cession and
most notab y,w hen MaryR amerman went to Orang ,C alifornia
to meet BishopP eter,s he repr ted that his commni tyof St Matthew p acticed and honored the v rys ame thing that Sp ritu
Christi did. Clearly,t his was the rigt p th for MaryR amerman,
b was it rigt for me? Unlik Mary, I was a cradle-br n Roman
Catholic,a nd while I had alway b en more of a Cafeteria Catholic I ju t wasn't sn e this was the p th for me. For so long had
said that I didn't feel called ou of the Catholic Chn ch to p su
ordination,b now I fond m y elf "k ck d ou " of that v ry
same Chn ch.I had learned and accep ed that there was Catholic
life ou side of the Roman Catholic Chn ch,b I was strg ing
to figure out if this was my path. BishopP eter was coming o
Sp ritu Christi Chn ch,s o I wrote to him abtu myc all,a nd my
nc ertainty,a nd ask d to meet with him one-on-one.

Our meeting was on a Friday after my noon communion service. Bishop Peter came to the service, and afterwards we went to lunch. We talked freely for quite some time. Bishop Peter explained his own journey and I shared mine. As lunch progessed he turned to me and said "Well Denise, I've read your call story and your letter, and as we've talked it is very clear to me that your call to ordination is genuine. It is also clear that you have a tremendous amount of support from your faith community. Now the decision is yours— the door is open. Will you walk through that door?"

Suddenly I had an out of body experience that brought me to four different points in my journey. I remembered my experience with John White, the spiritual medium. He had ended his message to me with the words," A time will come when Jesus will hand that staff to you and you will have a decision to make. Will you accept it or not? The choice will be yours."

Before I could even ask myself if this was that moment or not, I was transported to another moment in my journey when I was talking with my advisor at Colgate Rochester Divinity School. I told her that Bishop Peter was coming to town, and I was wondering whether this was meant to be my path to ordination or, as I had assumed for years, if I needed to wait for the possibility to present itself in the Roman Catholic Church. She had advised me to return to my original call: "Are you called to reform the Roman Catholic Church, or are you called to minister to the people?" I had immediately countered," Well, when you put it that way, it's very clear. I'm called to minister to the people, reforming the Church simply comes from the fact that the path to ordination is blocked for me.

As I sat with Bishop Peter the memories were coming into my awareness rapid-fire. I recalled a friend who told me she had a dream about me. In her dream I was trying to scale the walls around a purple castle. She told me there wasn't any visible means to get in, but I was determined. Over and over I would try to climb the walls, I would fall backdown, get up and try again.

She said my knees were all bloodied and I was in a lot of pain, but I just kept trying over and over again.

Finally, I remembered being with my spiritual director years previously. I had been questioning my call to ordination by mercilessly interrogating myself and my emotions. My spiritual director looked me right in the eye and said, "Denise, how many more times does God have to say *yes* to you before you stop questioning it?"

In these few moments at the table with Bishop Peter I had traveled across my life, while he had no way of knowing where I'd been. Suddenly he looked at me and said, "Denise, we're in the presence of the Holy One right here and now. The hair on the back of my neck is standing straight and look at the hair on my arms." As I looked back into his face he said, "I call moments like these 'Divine Visitations.' " I was astounded, and I finally said "YOU feel God's presence! You have no idea where I've just been!" From that moment on I've never questioned that this was the right path for me.

My ordination to the priesthood on February 28 was one of the happiest days of my life. All of my life I had felt this calling so deep within my soul. I had struggled to understand what it was, finally named it, spent all kinds of energy denying it, finally embraced it along with the pain of assuming it would never come to fruition, and now I was living it! Just a day before my ordination I woke up one morning with a song in my heart. As I wiped the grogginess from my eyes I realized the song was singing as "Everyday with you GOD is sweeter than the day before! Everyday I love you more and more, more and more and more. And when I get to sleep at night time tomorrow's what I'm waiting for, cause everyday with God is sweeter than the day, sweeter than the day, sweeter than the day before!" My soul and my spirit were carrying the joy within me, even when my body and mind were sleeping

In preparation for my ordination I was intimately aware of the women who had blazed a path before me, and those who were to come behind. I wanted to honor the sisters on who's shoulders I stood, so I asked Rev. Christine Mayr-Lmetzberfer, Rev. Kathy McCarthy, Rev. Gioanna Piazza and Rev. Mary Ramerman if I could use some aspect of their ordinations (a song, a reading, a payer, etc) within my ceremony, and honor them in my program. Rev. Kathy McCarthy (the first woman that Bishop Peter Hickman had ordained) had immediately told me, "You have to dance!!" I argued that unlike her, I was not a liturgical dancer, but she told me that liturgical dance is not about dance— it's payer that involves movement and song. At her insistence I danced to the song "Spirit of the Living God, Fall afresh on me." I knew that if I danced I was not going to be alone up here, so I asked my daughters, two of my closest friends and their daughters to join me in this dance. These were the women that had walked this journey with me. They had felt my tears and shared in everyone of my joy! And so we danced.

Years previously I had a dream about being in an "upper room" standing around a round table with other women, all in albs, celebrating Eucharist together. As I stood at the altar the next morning for my first Mass I asked my sister priests to join me, and we concelebrated together. At first people questioned me: "Denise, this is your first Mass—the first time you will be celebrating the Eucharist. Are you sure you want others at the altar with you?" In other words, are you sure you want to share the spotlight? My answer: Unequivocally YES! As women we don't walk our journey alone, and acknowledging, thanking and involving other women in our moments of joy never diminishes us—it only amplifies the joy and reflects the Holy Spirit. My ordination is not about me, it's about the movement of the Holy Spirit in our world. It's about God creating a way where there is no way. It's about standing in solidarity with those who came before and those who will come after!

In the week that followed, every time I celebrated the Eucharist people told me I looked so natural, like I'd been doing this for years. "I have," I'd say, "right here," as I'd point to my chest. That little girl who sat in the pews and had watched every move of the altar boy, had also watched every move of the priest. I knew the Eucharistic Prayers by heart and I often wondered why the priests looked so bored while they read the words, or why they panicked and stopped midstream when they turned to the wrong page. I remember thinking to myself, "This is such a beautiful prayer, why aren't they praying it from their heart?"

After my ordination I realized I had never felt more fulfilled in life. I had a beautiful family, terrific friends, and I served in a community that I loved. I always assumed I would be at Spiritus Christi until I retired, but that assumption changed in October, 2014. I was out on a medical leave, was one-week post-surgery, and despite having had major abdominal surgery, on that particular day I felt better than I had in years. My daughter stopped by to see me that night and as she came into the room she said, "Oh my God, Mom, you look fabulous! You look years younger, like you looked when I was in high school." While I felt really great, it was surprising to me that she could see it. After she left I turned out the light and began to pray. "Loving God, thank you! My life is so full and I am so blessed! I have a great husband, a beautiful family, terrific friends, and I love being a priest! But God, what am I going to do? I only have seven weeks left of my break." I stopped myself short—break? I was out on a medical leave, and I suddenly realized that perhaps it was time for me to move on. I loved my work but the amount of stress I experienced at Spiritus Christi was becoming too great and it was impacting my health. I started to cry, "God, what am I going to do?" The answer was immediate. "Start a new church." My response was sassy. "Oh, right God—just start a new church, like that's so easy! And where, pray tell, would I begin this new community?" Immediately I heard, "You've grown your whole life in

2

Fair prtt— here are people on the East Side, closer to home, that will never find their way to Spiritus Christi. But they also need to be fed." I spent the next three hours in prayer and tears, going around and around with God. Every time I raised an objection I would have a vision or hear an answer. I fell asleep that night feeling like Jacob who wrestled with the angel all night long.

My plans to stay at Spiritus Christi until my retirement were just that—my plans! Clearly God had something else in mind. I left my full-time position as Family Minister at Spiritus Christi Church on May, and that very evening with approximately twenty to twenty-five friends and family, we celebrated the Eucharist in our family room. This was the very first mass of what became Mary Magdalene Church. From the outside looking in, one might think I had jumped off a cliff—leaving a full-time position in ministry to begin something, and new with seemingly nothing, but there was so much peace in my heart that I knew this was the right thing.

By December, we found a building in East Rochester that had formerly been a credit union, with ample space for us to gather. As I said to the community, "Church is not about the building, it's about the people. We can create a sanctuary anywhere if we carry the spirit in our hearts." When the town was concerned about changing the building's zoning to public assembly because the parking lot was small, I said, "You don't understand. We're very small—so much so that we're creating a BYOC church." They asked me what a BYOC church was. "Bring Your Own Chair!" And so, in place of pews we had chairs of every imaginable. Everything from stacking chairs to plastic lawn furniture, but it's amazing what you can do with a few well-placed curtains and some room dividers. I often saw the look of pleasant surprise when people came in for the first time, and I loved to say, "Welcome to Mary Magdalene Church! We don't have much but all the other churches in town are jealous; they have their stained-glass windows, but we're the only church in town with a shut and a drive-through!" This building at Main Street in East Rochester served us well for more than three years, when the opportunity presented itself to move six blocks down Main Street to share space with Trinity Lutheran Church.

Trinity was struggling financially, and their congregation was quickly dwindling. While we had shared love, laughter, faith and sorrow in our make-shift church, when we moved in April, we were excited to move into a "real church." I knew it might be complicated to share space with another community, but this was sacred space, where the faith, love, prayers and intentions of others had been lifted-up for years, and that spirit already graced this sanctuary. By the time we moved in, Trinity's members had dwindled to only six or eight people at their weekly liturgies, and within a couple of months they discontinued their liturgies altogether.

As Trinity began moving toward the decision to disband, we began to think about the possibility of owning the building. In order to seriously consider this as an option, however, we needed to bring it to the community. We set up a meeting immediately after Mass on Sunday, July. It was a hot summer day and the front doors of the church were opened wide. Five minutes before Mass was to begin, we were all shocked when two mourning doves flew right into the sanctuary and perched on a window sill in the front of the church, just over the front door. They remained in that window until just after my homily, at which point the female swooped right down the center aisle and perched on the banner behind the large cross hanging on the altar. I assumed she would fly back to join her mate as soon as I invited everyone to join me at the altar for the consecration. On the contrary. She remained right there, just over my right shoulder, for the remainder of the liturgy. After Mass, as I stood at the lectern to begin the meeting, I announced that the only agenda item we had for our gathering was to discuss the possibility of pursuing the purchase of this church building. I looked past the door over my shoulder, and the one in the front window of the church, and said, "Does anyone have any questions?" It seemed pretty clear to all of us that we had the blessing of the Holy Spirit.

Our community has felt those blessings in numerous ways over our time together. While we are not large in numbers, with an average Sunday Mass of fifty to sixty people, we are very welcoming and inclusive, and what we lack in size we make up for in enthusiasm, commitment and generosity. In fact, the neighbors who have lived next door to the church for thirty plus years have frequently told us that even in its heyday, this church has never been as full of life and activity as it is now.

Between pastoring Mary Magdalene Church, having an active social and family life, and providing child care for my grandchildren two days a week, my plate was very full. The last thing I anticipated was adding another hat to the many that I wear. But as is so often the case in my spiritual life, just when I think I've "arrived" God has something else in mind.

In May I was invited, at the suggestion of Frank Krebs, the Presiding Bishop of the Ecumenical Catholic Communion (ECC), to be a part of a team of five women to address the issue of Women in the ECC at the upcoming synod. It was a huge undertaking for while we all knew that the ECC espoused the equality of all, and certainly supported the ordination of women, we also knew that inherent in everything from language to ritual to practice there has been an internalization of the patriarchy and clericalism that was a part of the Roman Church. One does not leave an institution with such a significant history of oppression and expect that we are now free from the '*isms* that were a part of its history. Throughout our preparation for synod, our notice, and workshops, there was one very obvious area where women were not represented, and that was in the episcopacy. There were no women bishops! While there had been two occasions in which women were among those nominated for an episcopal position, neither of them had been elected.

As I prepared for the synod I was anxious. I began to feel God working within me in ways I was very resistant to. You see, within the ECC several people had told me over the years that they could see me as a bishop or that the ECC needed me as a bishop. Every time it was raised I immediately and vehemently responded, "No way! No how! Look elsewhere!" I had absolutely no interest or desire. That was in part because I couldn't imagine how I would have the time (and I was not willing to give up anything else in my life), and partly because over the years I had been privy to some of the political struggles within the ECC, and I was averse to politics in church. Two of the guiding principles of Mary Magdalene Church, when we formed, were transparency and accountability, as I felt that when these were lacking there was a high probability that politics would come into play. I had watched some of the struggles within the ECC, especially between the more egalitarian principles that were a part of the founding of the organization, and those factions which had a very clerical bent and were focused on authority and "power." I had too much experience with this ugly side of religion from my day in Corpus Christi to tolerate any of it. In fact, for a long time I questioned my desire to remain connected to this organization. But there had been a rift within the ECC a few years previously, and those more clerically focused had broken away. Since that time I've experienced the ECC as a much more healthy organization, and one that I have highly valued.

At the end of the synod it was clear that there was a strong movement among those gathered to see women within the Episcopal Council, and Bishop Francis Krebs announced his intention to see a woman elected and ordained as bishop by the end of 2017. The group of women who had been invited to be part of addressing the issue of women in the ECC at the synod continued to meet in the months following and I knew it was just a matter of time before those who had previously nudged, suggested, and nudged me in this direction would again begin to beckon. I was prepared with all the excuses I could think of, until one day when I experienced a voice within me that startled me. "Denise, you have not once brought this to me in prayer!" Suddenly, I realized how true that was. Every single time someone had come to me, my response was a quick, knee-jerk reaction. I had not even allowed the suggestion to get inside of my awareness. I had never seriously considered it. I had never once asked God if this was a part of my call. Even as I began to bring this to prayer, my prayer was much more of an argument with God about how full my life was. I didn't have time, and without adequate time I would not be the best option for the Communion. But just as fervently as I had held this at arm's length, God began to work within my soul.

As I prayed I recalled something that had happened many years ago, when I was working at Corpus Christi Church. I was walking across the parking lot from my office to the rectory for a staff meeting when a bird, in fact a cardinal, whizzed by me so low that I actually ducked, and instantaneously the question popped into my head "I'm going to be a cardinal?!" Instantly I thought: "No, not a cardinal but a bishop." I remember shaking my head in disbelief, but I quickly disregarded it as a strange passing thought. At the time I had thought it was utterly absurd, and not only impossible but additionally incongruous with what I had come to believe to be my call, and I forgot all about it, until many moons later. I was sharing with my spiritual director this moment I was experiencing within me to consider being open to the call to be a bishop in the ECC. At one point in one conversation I was pensively looking out the sliding glass door when I spotted a cardinal perched on the limb of a tree in her backyard. Suddenly this memory came flooding back, and as I shared it with Dijana I felt chills go down my spine.

As I continued to process where I was feeling led in my spiritual life, I had a conversation with a friend about it, and she directed me to the experience I had had when I visited that spiritual medium who told me that Jesus had a staff for me. "You know," she said," the staff is a symbol of a bishop not a priest." I did of course realize it, but I had been trying to hold that realization at bay.

In the Fall of [?] an episcopal opening was announced in the ECC for an auxiliary bishop to serve as an assistant to Bishop Francis. I was not only nominated, but within thirty six hours I had received the endorsements of people from different regions of the United States. On Dec 1, [?] the results of the election were announced. I had been elected to the position of auxiliary bishop. Interestingly, that same week was the nineteenth anniversary of my being fired as Family Minister at Corpus Christi! What had seemed like such a dark day, a day I assumed would mean I'd never again be hired to work within a Catholic Church, had actually led to the opening of possibilities beyond my imagining.

As I prepared for my episcopal ordination I was forced to deal with my distaste for some of the symbols of office. Given my experience with the spiritual medium, it is probably a given that the crozier was easy for me—it is the symbol of the shepherd. It also became a very special symbol as my husband, who loves working with wood, made it for me. The pectoral cross was also very easy as I— wear a cross almost every day. Of course it is not nearly as [?] as the pectoral cross is only worn when vested in liturgy, it is very appropriate. In addition, my parents wanted to gift me with this symbol. The symbols I struggled with were the ring and the miter. My community, however, decided to give me the ring They wanted it to be a symbol of their love for me and indicated that I would "carry Mary Magdalene Church with me wherever I went."

The Miter, however, was a whole other bailiwick I was very opposed to it. I saw it as an imperial symbol and a symbol of distinction, and no one could give me a spiritual meaning for it that was satisfactory. I said on several occasions "You'll never see a miter on MY head!" It got to be a running joke between myself and my assistant pastor at Mary Magdalene Church, Rev. Philip Benier. In my sacrilege on him or I frequently said, "There will be no pointy hat for me!" One night as he and I were talking he said something to me that he had not said before. "Do not disdain the symbols of office, because those symbols are greater than you and convey a continuance with the historical Church. In those symbols of office people find meaning, an anchor." These words stopped me in my tracks. I had to let them in, and as I did, as is so often the case in my spiritual journey, the Holy Spirit used this time to help me look at some thing differently. As I prayed about it I remembered two things. The first came to me immediately— in fact I remembered it as soon as I read Philip's text. It was an experience that a dear friend and sister priest, Rev. Giovanna Piazza shared with me. When she was ordained her mother gave her a gold-plated chalice and paten. Giovanna said to her mother, "Mom, this really isn't me!" Her mother replied that the symbolism of the chalice was not for her. "It's for the people in the congregation. When you hold that gold chalice they can see how it shines, and they can see their own reflection."

The other memory that came to me was an experience I had shortly after my ordination. I was celebrating the noon mass one Friday, and when I came into the chapel I noticed a young woman I'd never seen there before, and she was crying. I wondered what had brought her in today, and imagined that she had maybe lost a grandparent, or had just gotten some bad news. At the sign of peace I sought her out, and the very first thing she said to me was, "I'm sorry. I can't stop crying. I've never seen a woman vested before and celebrating Eucharist." She went on to say that she was a photography student at the Rochester Institute of Technology. Then she added, "During the homily I started crying even harder. My photography project right now is to photograph someone in uniform, and I suddenly realized you were in your uniform!" As this memory returned to me in prayer I realized something very significant. If I refused to wear the miter, would

I b deny ngv omen the opr tni tyt o see a woman flu lyv sted for office? I would not be able to explain to people why I'm not wearinga miter,a nd how woli d theyi nterp et that for themselv s? Woli d some q stion whether or not I was "eq l" to my male cont erp rts?

Yet ag in, the HolyS p rit had op ned mye y s throg t he words of a tru ted friend. Yes,t his syn bl is g eater than I,a nd in it people find meaning. I also realized that it isn't what I wear or don't wear that is impr tant,b   how I wear it! The fact that it woli d b a woman wearing his miter woli d alreadys p ak volumes about how we are reimagining the Church. I finally settled on a cop e of thing .F irst,t hat if I was gi ng o wear a miter it had to b feminine and hm b e! I immediatelyc ontacted the woman who had made my chasuble for me fifteen years ago— Charlotte Barnard,w ho is a b au iflu artist. As she was liv ng in Florida,s he inul v d another friend,E ileen Georg ,a nd my miter b au iflu lym atches myc hasb e with p nka nd p p e hu s p inted within it.S econdly,I realized it was ex remelyi mpr tant that I b v sted with the miter for the consecration.I t needed to be clear that this was not a "second-tier" ordination. And finally, I realized that when I'm with other b shop who are wearinga miter I need to wear mine,b   when I'm alone,nl ess req sted jw hatev r commni tyor indiv da l I am celeb ating r seriv ng at the time,I will not don the miter.I t is myhop   that within the Ep scop l Conc il we will hav a conv rsation abu this,a nd that we will jointlyde cide to tak off on mitersb— I will need to wait nt il we are ab e to p ocess this tog ther.(Leav it to the first woman bishop in the ECC to change the dress code!)

On Feb   wo day after mys ix ieth b rthdaya nd ju t two weeks shy of my fifteenth anniversary as a priest, I was consecrated a b shop. While I had fogt ag inst this call for many y ars,a s I layp ostrate b fore the cross I ke w with ev ryp rt of myb ing hat this,i n fact,w as rigt where I was sps ed to b , and I was humbly filled with peace.

Since that time, I have had several experiences that have shown me the significance my consecration as a bishop has had for other women. The most striking experience was in Puebla, Mexico. I had accompanied Bishop Armando Ley and Bishop Francis Krebs on a trip to Mexico to meet some of the individuals who were considering becoming a part of the ECC. We stayed at a retreat center run by nuns. When we arrived the first night Bishop Francis went in first. He began conversing with the sisters, and one of them asked if I was his wife. Frank chuckled a bit and said, "No, this is Bishop Denise. She's our newest bishop in the ECC." I could see among the sisters a look of both surprise and excitement as they spoke quickly with Frank. When it was time to leave, Mother Olga gave a new stole to Bishop Armando and Bishop Francis. How sweet, I thought to myself. Then another sister came out carrying a beautiful white onyx ciborium. They were thrilled to share this beautiful gift with me and I immediately knew this visit had been very special to them. As women engaged in ministry, I'm certain they had never imagined that they would experience a woman priest, much less a woman bishop, and I believe they identified with me as a kindred spirit.

KATHLEEN'S CALL

Kathleen Gorman

When I was growing up I longed to be an altar girl, but girls weren't allowed. I was always so mesmerized by the Mass, and was so very jealous of my two older brothers who could serve as altar boys. I remember saying the Eucharistic prayers silently with the priest during Mass, and even ventured to "be the priest" by hiding in a closet as I "blessed" the elements! It is incredible to me that I had forgotten that memory until it came blazing back to me as I was sitting in one of my classes at the Iliff School of Theology in the fall of 0

I was the seventh of eight children, and we were the model of the devout Roman Catholic family. We didn't miss a Sunday or holyday. Even when we traveled we always made it to Mass. One time when traveling we were late to Mass and missed the Gospel, and so not only did we stay through that Mass, we had to stay for the next Mass because those were the rules. My dad would say, if you miss the Gospel, you've missed Mass.

I attended a Jesuit college, Spring Hill College in Mobile, Alabama, and continued being a devout Catholic attending daily Mass most days. I loved my Theology and Philosophy classes. My favorite class was a Philosophy course based on Elisabeth Kübler-Ross' book *On Death and Dying*. It was such a profound experience. But I was so focused on becoming a Certified Public Accountant (because that's what my dad said I should do) that the profound experience of that course became a distant memory.

During those college years I was confronted with my sexuality in a way that rocked my world. I realized I was gay and was devastated because, for my parents, being gay was one of the worst things that a person "could do." Yes, being gay was something people "did," not what they were. When my folks found out one of their favorite priests was gay, my mom's reaction was: "I sure hope his mom never knew." So, I was back in the closet for many years, struggling with my sexuality. The benefit of this struggle was that my relationship with Mother Mary became quite intimate. I would pray the rosary and talk to Mary while walking the levee. After years of doing this I was finally able to hear Mary's guidance as she gently kept reminding me that God doesn't make mistakes, that I am what I am, and that I must love myself.

After graduating from college I entered into the accounting profession with Coopers & Lybrand, gaining experience in audit, tax, and computer consulting. Three and a half years later I started my own accounting company, servicing small business needs. I became certified as a financial planner and started gravitating into investment management. In 2 was working with Wachovia Securities, and I started loathing the business, seeing the manipulation of the market and the manipulation of people's accounts. I had to jump ship even though I had no idea where to go. I tried substitute teaching but it didn't take long for me to know that wasn't the path I should take.

One of my dear friends, sensing my struggle, invited me to join her crew doing landscape architecture for the summer. Her clientele were primarily from the Broadmoor and Kissing Camels communities in Colorado Springs, Colorado, so the work we did was extensive: tearing wood, moving heavy boulders, the work! It was during that time, one summer day, that I had the epiphany that would change the course of my life. I remembered how much I loved Elisabeth Kubler-Ross's book, and reflected on the volunteer activities that I was currently involved with, which included being a companion for the dying at the Mount Saint Francis Nursing Home, and taking cancer patients to their chemo and radiation appointments. I basically stopped in my footsteps as I thought, I want to be a hospice chaplain! And I knew, without a shadow of a doubt, that that's what I was born to do. So I enrolled in the Iliff School of Theology to earn my Master of Divinity degree at the age of forty-five.

But before going any further, I have to explain that this change from a financial career to becoming a hospice chaplain would never have happened had another miracle not surfaced in my life when I was thirty-three years old—in the midst of my accounting success, in the midst of struggling with my sexuality, in the midst of trying to figure out what my life was all about. I was on a business trip when a meditation book landed in my lap. It was an irony that I didn't toss the book aside and judge it as a New Age fad, because I was still quite the devout Catholic. The book was called *Passage Meditation*, by Eknath Easwaran. I read the entire book in one sitting, that night. The words reverberated through every cell of my body as I realized that I was a tripe A+ heart attack waiting to happen, that I had lived my entire life to please my parents, and that I had no idea who I was. As I was sobbing from this realization I surrendered to God and committed to devoting thirty minutes a day to meditation, knowing I had no idea where this practice would lead me. This spiritual practice has been my anchor for the past twenty-five years, and everyday I offer a prayer of gratitude for that October day in that I read Easwaran's book. That was the day that my little "elephant" eyes started expanding and including a bigger, more loving God of hope and promise and love and joy.

Four months later, two other miracles arrived in the form of puppies! In hindsight, these two black Lab ador puppies were my pastoral caregivers helping me navigate through many tumultuous times. I named one K (for Kathleen's Dog) and my partner named K's sister Foster. The first few years of meditating were like living through a tsunami as my entire theological foundation crumbled. I was so sure of what I believed prior to meditating. Subtle changes and beliefs kept happening until one year I could actually feel in the depths of my soul that the shackles and chains of judgment and self-righteousness were being unlocked and I was able to throw them overboard. Trust me, this doesn't mean that I no longer am judgmental or self-righteous at times! These are deep samskaras (roots) but with meditation, they are much less prevalent! On January 5th, my mom was diagnosed with lung cancer and died two weeks later on January 31st. This loss felt as if the umbilical cord was cut and I had nothing on which to anchor. It was during this period of time that I understood just how important K and Foster were to me. Their unconditional love and pure devotion to me was the salve that helped me stay the course of sanity— they were my anchor and they got me through life up to the time when I began seminary. Foster died in June and K died in March.

I loved my time at Iliff (starting my studies in January. I continued to do accounting work to get myself through college. In the fall of took the Hebrew Bible class that was required for the Master of Divinity degree. The first thing we did was introduce ourselves. We were asked to share which degree we were pursuing, where we were from, and which community we were a part of. During that process I heard two women declare they were Ecumenical Catholics. Ecumenical Catholics?

My ears perked because I had never heard of such a community. And, at that time in my life, I had abandoned the Roman Catholic Church because of its handling of the pedophile priests. I noted who those two women (Sheila Dierk and Teri Harroun) were, and during a break in class, asked them what they meant about being Ecumenical Catholics. They asked where I lived, then told me there was an Ecumenical Catholic Community very close by ..so I went there and found my home.

In the fall of 2012 as I was sitting in one of my classes a long-buried memory started reawakening. I gasped in the middle of class as I remembered hiding in the closet and "being" a priest, blessing the elements. Chills went up and down my spine as I realized that I had actually been called a long time ago. I couldn't help but tear up as I remembered how I felt as that little child. I remembered the reverence with which I blessed the elements, and how carefully I recited the Eucharistic prayers. I immediately contacted my priest from the little Ecumenical Catholic Community that I was attending and, well, the rest is history.

I was first ordained a deacon with Teri Harroun in September of 2013 and then ordained a priest on my forty ninth birthday. Assumption Day! I picked that day to be ordained a priest because I wanted my first Mass as priest and celebrant to be on The Feast of the Assumption of Mary. She has provided and continues to provide special guidance to me, and I couldn't imagine a better way to honor her as I accepted my calling as a priest.

I am energized each day as I seem to become more whole and more authentic. The love in my heart continues to expand to include all of Creation, and I feel so blessed by the many people in my life who have been cairns on this journey. I would be remiss if I didn't mention my spouse and beloved partner Tracy who has been an essential part of this journey as she continues to nurture and encourage me to have a voice and to honor that voice. To her and to all the special people who have been positive beacons of light, I am eternally grateful.

This isn't a story I share with my dad (my mom died in '9 , as she would declare me a heretic. Being a Catholic priest would be worse than being gay (which he doesn't accept either). Nor do I share this story with my seven siblings. The majority of them "hate the sin, love the sinner" regarding my sexuality, and I think they would feel that I've lost my marbles, daring to be a Catholic priest. And yet I have an intimate compassion for their perspectives, as I had those same perspectives for thirty-three years.

My heart would melt if they had an authentic desire to witness me as I celebrated Mass. But, my heart beats with the pulse of the Cosmos, and is touched each time I see a woman in the crowd tear up as she witnesses me, a woman Catholic priest celebrating Mass.

Y'ALL COME

Bridget Mary Meehan

When I reflect on my memories of an Irish childhood I realize that the Catholic Church is in my DNA. From my earliest years I experienced a call to serve God, first as a nun in traditional religious life and later, as that call evolved, to serve the people of God as a priest, and the international Roman Catholic Women Priests Movement as a bishop

I was born in Ireland, in 1948 into a warm and loving family. We lived in a little gray cottage in Coolkerry, a rural area outside Rathdowney, where cows and sheep grazed in green fields across from the Erkina River. In this peaceful place, our family fished and played in its shallow, cool water. We did not have many toys, but the earth was our playground. I molded and shaped mud pies in the rich moist soil of our garden. I imagined that my baked gods were culinary delights like my mother's rhubarb, ripe, scones and cake bread! I loved to feel the wind blowing in my hair as I walked through the fields dotted with daisies, buttercups, golden wildflowers and purple heather. I played hide and seek in hay stacks with school chums, and hunted for eggs that the hens laid in on bushes. The milk we drank came from one cow.

We had an open hearth and Mom always had a kettle on the boil, and every day we ate delicious home-made soda bread. My brother Patrick who was a year and one-half younger, and I walked home from school through the fields. We often stopped at Vester Campion's on the way out of Rathdowney for "sweets" (penny candy or ice cream wafers) which I put on Dad's tab.

Sean, my youngest brother, was born in D... Dad worked at the bank as a porter and played in Billy Ryan's band on weekends. On Sundays Dad took us for walks through the lovely countryside, and as we strolled leisurely along he told us enchanted stories of fairies, banshees, rabbits and badgers. Each story, which introduced us to the mystical magic of the Celtic spirit, began the same way." A long long time ago in Ireland"...

My grandfather, Pat Beale, was a gentle, quiet man who often watched Patrick, Sean and I when we were small children. He took us out to pet Neddy, our donkey, and we watched as Mom milked the cow. Patrick and I had a pet lamb that we fed with a bottle. One time the lamb swallowed the nipple from the bottle, and we ran to tell Mom this tale of woe. She assured us that all would be well. The lamb did not get sick and we learned our lesson. Each day we drew water from a well near the river, and used rain water to bathe. On Saturday evening it usually included warm baths in large tubs placed on the kitchen floor. Dad and Mom worked as a team. One washed us the other dried us, then off to bed. Even though we did not have central heat, just an open fire place and hot water bottles for our beds, I never remember being cold.

On Sundays, Grandfather yoked the pony to the trap and went to first Mass, then Mom and Dad went to second Mass. One time when Grandfather was minding us, he fell asleep and the three of us had great time with the flour. When Mom and Dad came home, the flour was all over the floor. Later they discovered that Grandfather was not feeling well. However, he gave exact instructions to my parents about "his last wishes." He told them that he was at peace, and that they were to treat everyone well at the wake, have lots of food and drink for all who came. He even told them that he wished to be buried in the new cemetery near the town, not in Hamnacart where his wife was laid to rest. Then, after a brief illness, Grandfather died and was laid out in his own habit in his own bed. People came from miles around to his all-day and all-night wake. They remembered Pat telling stories, laughing, crying and toasting him as they enjoyed delicious food and drink. I still remember how peaceful he looked lying there on his bed. I spent the night of the wake and funeral day with neighbors. As the funeral procession passed by, I counted the cars and thought that he must have been well-loved because such great crowds came to say farewell.

Our family was known as the musical Meehans, and our home was always filled with the sound of music. Dad's father, Grandfather Jack Meehan, was one of the founding members of the Ballyloan Band in the late 1800's and his sons, my dad, John (also called Jack), Jimmy, and Paddy all played in this band. Dad was a gifted musician who has played with many bands during his seventy-five year career, and during his retirement years he played both trumpet and saxophone for our inclusive Catholic liturgies and social gatherings in Florida and Virginia, until he passed into the fullness of God's embrace in 2009.

Ours has always been a praying family. In Ireland we gathered around the turf fire each evening to recite the rosary. My mother was a firm believer in the saying that a family that prays together, stays together. I had a sense early on that heaven and earth were closely connected, and the saints, angels, the Blessed Mother, and Jesus were family members who lived in heaven. I fell in love with God at a young age, and sensed that God was very fond of me, and close to everyone, including all creatures great and small.

I attended senior infants and first class in the National School in Rathdowney. The Sisters of St. John of God taught there, and I remember being slapped on my hand with a ruler when I answered a question incorrectly. In Irish schools at that time this was standard operating procedure, and I often had knots in my stomach for fear of being truly the ruler. Obviously, school was not a fun place!

Early on I was inspired by St. Brigit of Kildare, my patron saint. The stories about her blend Christian beliefs and pagan myths. St. Brigit was named after the Druidic mother goddess of fertility and abundance in ancient Ireland. St. Brigit saw to it that there was more than enough food, drink and love to nourish all who came to her hearth and home. No person who was poor or without resources ever left her presence without sustenance. Brigit even gave the feast day vestments of Bishop Conleth to the poor. In Trinity Church in Rathdowney, where I celebrated my first communion, there is a beautiful stained glass window of St. Brigit, dressed in purple, holding a pastoral staff.

According to *The Irish Life of St. Brigit*, Bishop Mel, who was St. Patrick's nephew, ordained Brigit a bishop. As the story goes, Bishop Mel said, "Come, O holy Brigit, that a veil may be placed on your head before the other virgins." Then, filled with the grace of the Holy Spirit, the bishop read the form of ordaining a bishop over Brigit. While she was being consecrated, a brilliant fiery glow ascended from her head. MacCaille, Bishop Mel's assistant, complained that a bishop's rank was bestowed on a woman. Bishop Mel argued: "But I do not have any power in this matter. That dignity has been given by God to Brigit, beyond every other woman." Indeed, other bishops sat at the feet of Brigit's successor until the Synod of Kells ended the practice in 1152. This monastic bishop was peculiar to Irish law, and indicated the powerful positions of abbots and abbesses of the great monasteries.

According to tradition St. Brigit built her monastery in Kildare near a large oak tree in 480 A.D. Both Brigit of Kildare and Hilda of Whitby founded monasteries in which women and men lived, some as celibates, and others as married couples with children, but all living in Christian community having dedicated their lives to Christ. In the sixth century, three Roman bishops sent a letter to two Breton priests, Lovocat and Cathern, banning women from presiding at Mass: "You celebrate the divine sacrifice of the Mass with the assistance of women. . . . While you distribute the Eucharist, they take the chalice and administer the blood of Christ to the people. . . . Renounce these abuses." My passion for justice and equality for women in the church is rooted in my Celtic soul that draws its inspiration from my patron saint, Brigit of Kildare (from Olie r Dai s,e ditor of *Celtic Spirituality,* c ited in Meehan, *Praying with Celtic Holy Women,* p).

Arria l and Settling n the US A

In June, w e emig ated to the United States. It took seven days to cross the stormy north Atlantic. As we sailed into New York Harbor the majestic Statue of Liberty stood as a beacon of welcome to our new home. We were awestruck by the skyscrapers that loomed ahead of us, and felt the heat of the sun beating down on us. Then, the next day we drove to Philadelphia to feast with our cousins who had emigrated from Ireland decades before. After this delicious meal we drove to our new home in Arlington, Virginia, where we settled in quickly. Dad went to work in a maintenance job in the DC Public Schools, and was invited to join a local band that played for the Irish Club in DC. Mom, a home-maker, took care of Sean, prepared us for school, and babysat for a few young children in our home.

I still remember my first year at Saint Thomas More School as a tram atic ep rience.I was a chu little girl with cn ly hair. At recess, some of my classmates wou d tease me abu the way I talked. Some called me "fatso" and wou d not

let me join in their g mes. I often cried, coυ dn't concentrate in
school, and felt as if I didn't belong. I did not begin to flourish
in my new env ronment nt il the fon th g ade, when a loν ly,
g ntle nn , Sister Marita Loυ se, eϸ essed her b lief in me.
My sϸ rit soared,m y g ades imp oν d,a nd I made new friends.
Affirmations always build us up.

I attended Bishop Denis J. O'Connell High School, and for
the most part, I enjoyed the experience. For me, high school was
a time of serious study and reaching out—doing service projects
in clubs, like putting on a party for children with special needs.
Music and laughter is the common language of the soul that con-
nects us beyond our limitations. I felt that God was calling me to
consecrate my life to service, but I struggled with the nun bit. Me,
a nun? You have got to be kidding! I enjoyed life too much.

After viewing the movie "The Nun's Story," the idea of
convent life repelled me. So I had some heart-to-heart conversations with God in which I did most of the talking. There was no
way that I was going to scrub a floor, like the submissive nun did
in the movie, and let someone deliberately walk all over it! So I
applied and was accepted at George Mason University, but in the
end I made a deal with God that if I found religious life to be like
"The Nun's Story," I'd be out of there!

Pilg imag s to oυ Homeland

We returned to Ireland several times, always to a warm
welcome from our extended family. On one of our vacations
in Ireland our family was having a great time in Ballyheigue, a
scenic town on the western coast of Ireland. One windy summer's evening, when everyone else was at tea, I took a walk by
myself. I was feeling anxious about a major change in my life. As
I strolled along the ocean's edge, the majestic waves were breaking at my feet and a strong wind at my back was propelling me
forward. Clouds floated across the evening sky, shapes shifting
as they drifted effortlessly by, and the crimson sunset painted the

horizon with golden red hues. I felt a peace descending on me. In the depths of my soul I heard God assuring me, "I will love you forever, with all my love." At that moment I knew that no matter what happened, all would be well. Words are inadequate to express how deeply I felt God's love surrounding me. It was a mystical experience, and is, to this day, one of the most powerful spiritual experiences of my life.

Visiting or reminiscing about the places that have been significant in our lives is often helpful and affirming. Some people make spiritual pilgrimage to the houses that have been home for them in the past. I made such a visit to the three-room cottage where I and my two brothers, Patrick and Sean, spent our earliest years together with our grandfather, Papa Beale. I walked to the spring where we drew water from the well. Then I went to Grogan, to the church, now boarded up where Mom and Dad were married fifty years ago. I sat in the church in Rathdowney where I made my first holy Communion, right under the stained-glass window of Saint Bridget. I stopped at Lady's Well, where Dad's band would pray every year on the feast of the Assumption, and from where we always carried home bottles of blessed water. My last stop was the cemetery outside Ballyroan, to place my hand on the tombstone of Grandfather and Grandmother Meehan. These kinds of journeys affirm our very existence by putting us in touch with our roots. We stand on the shoulders of those who have gone before us. There is a thin veil between this world and the next, and all of life is laden with grace—both in our times of joy and our times of sorrow. Our loved ones who have gone before us, who are now members of the communion of saints, stand ever ready to help us. They rest in the eternal embrace and are but a prayer away.

The Convent and Beyond

I frequently attended daily Mass in grade school, and there experienced a special closeness to Jesus in the Eucharist. The call

5

to priesthood, to celebrate the sacred in sacramental encounters and liturgical prayer, I believe, was imbedded in my soul in those early years of my life. But I could not name it yet, so I started the journey on the road traditionally set aside for women called to serve God is service not hers.

After graduation from Bishop O'Connell High School I entered the Immaculate Heart of Mary Sisters. There were ninety postulants who entered the convent on September 15, 1966. The new motherhouse was still a work in progress so there were workers all over the building who provided a major distraction. We learned how to make tight beds that you could bounce a quarter on, and when one Postulant director did not know what to do with us, she sent us to bush our teeth. Our rooms were separated by partitions and curtains. At night we were supposed to finish our day in sacred silence and our last act was to pray prostrate on the ground. Well, the first night I prostrated the wrong way. I wondered what the giggling was about! I have so many wonderful memories of our band, the group I entered with forty four years ago. We had a reunion four years ago at Stone Harbor for both the "ins" and "outs."

I am grateful for the ten years I spent as an IHM Sister. I learned a great deal about the spiritual life and about the gift of consecrated life. In 1977, after my mother had serious back surgery, I took a leave of absence to help care for her. It was during this time that I realized that traditional religious life was no longer a good fit for me. This began a lengthy process of discernment that included prayer, reflection and conversations with companions on the journey and different religious communities. Finally, in 1996, I joined Sisters for Christian Community, a prophetic ecclesial community of consecrated women "living a commitment to serving the people of God in a 'new pattern of the consecrated life that is self-determining, self-regulating, self-governing.'" There is no category in the institutional church to define us.

Our vision is to strive for a community of equals and to live the prayer of Jesus "that all may be one."

Pastoral Ministry

Throughout the years I became aware that other denominations were ordaining women, and I pledged myself to work for ordination of women in the Roman Catholic Church. I strongly sensed God's call to priesthood when I worked for fifteen years as a pastoral associate at Ft. Myer Chapel in Arlington, Virginia. I did everything except preside at Mass and sacraments. Often, when I conducted a communion service in the absence of a Catholic priest, the people would express their gratitude for the "lovely Mass." Even though I made it clear that this was a Communion Service, they often called it a Mass. So it dawned on me that they would easily accept me as their priest if I were ordained.

I often prepared copies for marriage, but the chaplain, who did not know the couple, officiated at their wedding. Some of the chaplains that I worked with would have been delighted if I could have officiated at weddings and in anointing the sick. They had so many duties with the military that they would gladly have shared the ministry with me. So my call to priestly ministry, over the years, was gradually confirmed by this wonderful community that I dearly loved, and by several communities that I have served over the past twelve years. One of these communities in Northern Virginia met for twelve years to reflect on the Sunday Scripture readings in preparation for liturgy.

In 2006 I was invited by a group of women from different faith traditions to lead discussions on women of the Bible. During one of these sessions I shared that I was invited to attend the first North American ordinations of Roman Catholic Women Priests, on the St. Lawrence Seaway. The women were delighted and told me that not only should I attend, but that I should be ordained and that they wanted me to be their priest! One woman even donated her frequent flyer miles so I could fly free to Canada.

I was awestru k n Gananoq y he ordination ceremony, and ke w that this was the p th God was callingn e to.S oon after,I ap lied and was accep ed as a candidate.I comþ eted the p eþ ration p og am,w hich consisted of ten ni ts of sacramental and þ storal theolog .I n addition,I hav a Doctorate in Ministry from Virg nia Eþ scop l Seminarya nd Master of Arts in Reli- g oa Stdi es from Catholic Univ rsityi n Washing on DC.

On July 31, 2006, I was one of twelve women ordained by three women bishops, Patricia Fresen, Gisela Forster, and Ida Raming, in Pittsburgh, on the river boat "Majestic." My dad, my brother Patrick, my soul friends Sister Regina Madonna Oliver, Peg Bowen, and several more beloved friends attended. As the bishops and people laid hands on us, I felt the Spirit's presence surrounding us in our prophetic witness for women's equality in the 21st century. Like the women who followed Jesus, Roman Catholic Women Priests are leading the Church to a new era of Gospel inclusivity and partnership. A new day was dawning for the Catholic Church as twelve women walked into history, shook up the male hierarchy, and challenged sexism in the church. By offering a renewed model of priestly ministry in a community of equals, women priests ignited a revolution in the Roman Catholic Church.

PriestlyM inistryB eg ns

Mym other,B ridie,ha d mont ain-moiv ngf aith and was alway flu l of wisdom,e ncon aig ngn e to g ow sþ ritu lly.S he did not liv to see me ordained,b I kow her p ay rs contin- a to enfold me and streng hen myf aith. When we rememb r on lov d ones who hav crossed ov r into God's emb ace,t hey b come p esent to a .I b liev that there is a clod of witnesses, myf amilya nd friends who hav gne b fore me,c heeringn e on from heav n.M ye igt y eigt y ar-old dad,J ack, a b gs þr ter of Roman Catholic Women Priests,c ontina s to b ess me as I þ ay ecording of his joya rendition of "When the Saints g

Marching n" at memorial seriv ces.M yb others,P atricka nd Sean and their families are spr tiv of myc alling n many way ,t heyk epm e g onde d in reality, and remind me that the chang that I hav dedicated mye nerg o maynot hap n in my lifetime.

Before gi ng o Florida in fD ad and I met with the PAX commni ty, an established Northern Virginia Roman Catholic commni tyw ho hav hired their own p iests for fy ars and þ anned their litn g es with these p esiders. Theya sk d me to p eside at their Thank g iv ng itn yb cas e theyf elt theyw ere readyf or a woman p iest. A litn g eam met with me for two hon s to p ep re this litn g .I wore a stole at their req st and we celeb ated the litn g n a larg room in a hon e.P eoþ e sang joyn ly,s hared op nlya nd p rticip ted flu ly.

Soon after Dad and I retn ned to Florida,m emb rs of on hon e chn ch b g n to g ther on Satn daye v ning and warm-lyw elcome one another.D ad þ ay d a p ocessional hyn n,l ik "AmazingG race," on the saxw ith a wee b t of jazz,t hat drew all of n into the sp rit of p aise for on Satn daye v ningM ass at Mary, Mother of Jesus House Church. Our fledging community sanga nd op ned on hearts to one another as we shared stories of on faith liv s dn ing he shared homily,a nd recited the Eu haristic Pray rs tog ther." Do this in memoryof me" we p ay d and so we tookJ esn ' words literallya s we celeb ated tog ther the my teries of on faith at the sacred b nq t. As devtn Roman Catholics hav done throg t he ag s in their local chn ches,w e, the Bodyof Christ,a re sharing he Eu harist,t he Bodyof Christ, with the Bodyof Christ. We,t he g thered assemb y,c eleb ate on my tical oneness with Christ with all the saints,w ho hav gne b fore n and with the þ lg im p oþ e of God,t he entire chn ch.

The onlydi fference is that I am a Roman Catholic Woman Priest p esiding n a chn ch that has y t to accep women's ordi-nation,e v n thog w omen serv d the Christian commni tyi n ordained ministry during its first twelve hundred years (see Gary

Macy, *The Hidden History of Women's Ordination,*a nd Ute
Eisen , *Women Officeholders in Early Christianity*).O n en-
erg zed incls ie commni ty s not waiting or p rmission from
chn ch atu horities. As one woman noted," The Vatican will catch
pone of these day ." Until then,w e said: "Let's p aise God yu
holyp ob e with holym s ic." And so we did ee ryw eeki n the
winter in on cozyhom e onlya few miles from the Gh f of Mek -
co from 9 9

Celeb atingL itn y n Hos e Chn ches

There are millions of Catholics,a ccording o sn e y ,w ho
hae left the chn ch for one reason or another.I t is myhop to
offer them a warm welcome home! Since I am Irish yb rth,
offeringho sp talityi s p rt of myc h tn al inheritance. We are
p ob e-friendly.O n litn g es are festie , fh l of songm s ic,
clap ngs ing nga nd ee n sway ngnow and ag in! One woman,M arie,w ho had b en dior ced and remarried,c ried when
she receie d commni on at on hos e chn ch last sp ing After
a hostile encont er with a p iest y ars ag,s he felt nw orthy o
receie the Eu harist in her p rish commni ty.N ow she said:
"I feel lik I hae come home at last." Marie has inv ted me to
celeb ate Mass in her home nek season in Florida. I þ an to do
"home Masses" when p ob e ask When p ob e are sicka nd
infirm, I gather with their family and friends in their own sur-
rondi ng o administer the sacrament of the anointingof the sick
in a commna l setting niv tingot hers to also anoint and p ay
tog ther for healinga nd wholeness.

In the 2 t centn y,C atholic worship,c entered in the Eu haristic thank -g iv nga nd self-g iv ngof Jesn ,i s once ag in b ing
celeb ated in hos e chn ches. Roman Catholic Women Priests are
leading he wayt o reclaim the ancient tradition of Eu haristic
tab e-sharing hat h lds commni ty.L ik the holyw omen and
men of the earlyc hn ch,w e are g thering og ther to b eakop n
on lie s,t o share b ead and wine in memoryof Jesn ,a nd to lie

the Christ-Presence in our work for justice, peace and equality in our world.

Therefore, it is appropriate that the community, not the priest alone, say the words of consecration together. Gary Macy, chairperson of the Theology and Religious Studies Department at the University of San Diego, concludes that, in the understanding of the medieval mind, regardless of who spoke the words of consecration—man or woman, or dained or community—the Christ presence became a reality in the midst of the assembly.

Roman Catholic Women Priests are dreaming daring dreams and discovering fresh visions. Jack Duffy, one of our Sarasota House Church members shares what it means to worship in spirit and truth as the Body of Christ: "In this small, intimate, friendly, around- the-table setting, the worship was deeply spiritual, holy. We could all really sense that Jesus was there with us. The Masses celebrated by Bridget Mary, a validly ordained Roman Catholic priest, were no different from those we have attended done by other validly ordained male priests. Her ordination was completely valid; as are the Masses at which she officiates. Having a woman priest may seem 'new' and radical; however, it is fairly certain that women and married men had been the ones presiding at the Eucharistic celebrations in the early Christian Church. So when the Roman Catholic Church finally evolves to this 'new' and radical way of operating it isn't really new at all. A prominent US Catholic Bishop from Detroit speaking here in Sarasota two weeks ago predicted the Church of the future will most likely see married and female priests."

Yes, indeed, we have come full circle. Like our sisters and brothers in the early Christian community, we bless and share the sacred meal, in Mary, Mother of Jesus Catholic Community House Church. We believe that Christ is calling us to go forth, filled with God's love and compassion to minister as partners and equals with all God's people. The world is our parish and, as my Southern neighbors say, y'all come!

MaryM other of Jesu Inclu iv Catholic Commni ty

In M aryM other of Jesu Catholic Commni tyde cided to rn a n ad in the local *Sarasota Herald Tribune*,i niv ting a ll to attend a week y,i nclu iv Catholic Mass in on hou e chn ch, which still,a t that pi nt,m et in myhom e. The Roman Catholic Diocese of Venice respnde d immediately. Theya sk d the *Herald-Tribune* to stopr nni ng his relig ous seri ce annonc ement, b the editors decided not to comp y.

It was the "snowb rd season" when p op e came to Florida to enjoy he sns hine and escap the cold weather.I receiv d lots of phone calls,a nd each weekm ore p op e crowded into myt iny liv ng oom for Mass.O n sev ral occasions we had to br row on neibor 's chairs. Then p rk ng came a p ob em b cau e there were too manyc ars on on street and the Association ask d that we p rk n a lot abu a half-mile away,w hich meant ol n - teers would do traffic control and shuttle people back and forth from the p rk ng ot to on mob le home. We continu d to þ ace on ad in the newsp p r. Then the diocese þ aced an annonc e- ment in the Herald-Tribe stating hat "no su h worships ite ek sts within the Diocese,nor is it recogi zed þ he Diocese of Venice" (see article "Relig ou Frad or Relig ou Coniv ction," þ Tom Lyons, *Sarasota Herald Tribune*,F e .

After sev ral letters of p otest from on commni tyw ere published in the newspaper, ABC TV showed up and filmed a Mass in on home. Theyi nteriv ewed JackD fi fy,a memb r of on commni ty,w ho said: "A chn ch lik Ep þa nyC athedral is so b ga nd hg ,b this is more p rsonal,m ore intimate and we can feel a little more tit er relationshipw ith Jesu ....I can see where officials in the Catholic church might not approve of it, but as my wife so clearly says, we are spirit-filled, common-sense Catholics. This ju t mak s sense."

The ABC interiv ew qt ed mya rgn ent that on Roman Catholic Women Priests initiativ was g onde d in Gosp l equality and early church history "Jesus was a rule breaker and he got in plenty of trouble for breaking the rules....Most people do not know that women were deacons, priests, and bishops and were ordained for the first 1200 years of their history. When they discover that they are simply taken aback.

Adela Gonzales White, a spokesperson for the Diocese of Venice stated: "Bridget Mary Meehan and her house church are not associated with the Catholic Diocese of Venice" ("Sarasota woman says she's a Catholic priest," ABC/Suncoast, March 5,). After the program aired, the Diocese took out ads listing Sunday Liturgies inside their Diocese.

Regardless of their intent, our community tripled in size. As a result we needed to move our Saturday evening liturgies from my home to a larger home. After three weeks, we outgrew the larger home and found a warm and welcoming sacred space at St. Andrew United Church of Christ. There we hold our Saturday evening liturgies at 6 pm. All are welcome to receive Eucharist at the banquet of Christ's love at Mary Mother of Jesus Catholic Community.

From to our community has continued to grow. We now have approximately fifty members during the winter season and thirty members during the off-season months. The entire community has an annual meeting at which all members gather to set policy, make decisions and approve our annual bud-get. We now have six women and two men who are priests who preside at liturgies.

Historic Florida Ordinations:

I was ordained a bishop on April . One of the high-lights of my first year as Bishop was the historic Florida ordinations. In Dec. our Mary Mother of Jesus community hosted the first diaconate ordinations in St. Andrew Church. Joining us were members of our sister-church, Good Shepherd Community in Ft. Myers, with their RCWP pastor, Judy Lee, who is also the

administrator of the Soũ hern Reḡ on of RCWP.D ena O'Cal-
laḡa n and KatyℤZ atsicḱt he ordinands for the Diaconate,w ere
accompa nied ṱt heir families.

On Feb. 5, 2010 we celebrated the priestly ordinations of Dena
and Katy, and the diaconate ordination of Mary Ellen Sheehan from
Georgia. The diocese of Venice announced that all who attended
the ordination would be excommunicated. Actually, the bishop's
threat (*Sarasota Herald Tribune* article reported by Anna Scott on
Feb. 6th, 2010) increased our attendance. Several people told us
they came to be in solidarity with the women being ordained, and
to support our justice movement for women in a renewed priestly ministry in our church. The people of God seem to regard this
punishment as a badge of honor. Over 250 people gathered in the
jam-packed church. All of the courageous Catholics who attended
this ordination, and all our supporters and communities are together
breaking the stained glass ceiling in the Roman Catholic Church.
The good news is that these Catholics are speaking truth to power
by their presence and support of our ordinations.

On May2 ,9ℬ he Vatican stated that anyw oman who
soḡt ordination,or a b shopẉ ho conferred holyor ders on
her,w oũ d b immediately" pi shed with ex ommni cation."
It went a step fṉ ther in ℂ ategr izinga nys ṳ h attempt as
delicta graviora -a- g aṿ crime aḡ inst the chṉ ch ₊— he same
categr ya s p iests who seᵈx llya ḅ e children (Leⅈ tt ℙ .

My Response to Vatican Decree of Excommunication: Disbelief

The Vatican has a lonḡhi storyof ex ommni catinḡ nter-
dictinḡa nd ṗi shingᴘ oṗ e in one centṉ ya nd canonizinḡ hem
in another centṉ y.P oṗ Benedict canonized Mother Theodore
Gṳ rin,a n ex ommni cated nṉ,i n ℬh nd will canonize
Mother MaryM acKilloᴘa nother ex ommni cated nṉ,i n ℚ
Mary Ward,a foṉdr ess of a reliḡ oᴎ order modelled on the
Jesuits, was vilified by church authorities. She was imprisoned at

one point, and recently has been declared Venerable, a step on the path to sainthood. One, of course, cannot forget St. Joan of Arc, patron of France, who rejected giving assent to church authorities and followed her conscience. She was burned at the stake and later declared a saint! St. Thomas Aquinas, one of the Church's greatest theologians, was excommunicated after his death!

The Vatican states that we are excommunicated, however, we do not accept this and affirm that we are loyal members of the Church. We continue to serve on below ground Church in a renewed priestly ministry, welcoming all to celebrate the sacraments in inclusive, Christ-centered, Spirit-empowered communities wherever we are called. There are approximately 8 anon women priest communities in 35 states and in Germany, Austria, France, Scotland, Canada, and South America. From our birth on the Danube River, RCWP has evolved into two streams in Europe (West and East), two in Canada (West and East), and two in the United States (RCWP USA and ARCWP).

The specific charism of ARCWP within the broader global Roman Catholic Women Priests initiative is to live Gospel equality and justice for all including women in the church and in society now. We work in solidarity with the poor, exploited, and marginalized for structural and transformative justice in partnership with all believers. Our vision is to act as a community of equals in decision-making both as an organization and within our faith communities. We advocate for the renewal of Jesus' vision as found in the Gospel for our church and our world.

As Pope Francis considers the possibility of ordaining women deacons in the Roman Catholic Church, I believe that our focus needs to be on the full equality of women in the priesthood and in all decision-making roles in the church. Equality is a basic human and spiritual right and the only way to heal centuries of toxic patriarchy.

This vision and mission has become the passion of my life! http://bridgetmary blog spot com/ mary mother-of-je-sus -inclusive -catholichtml

THE BEST THING

Kae Madden

O God who dwells within me –S oar!
Break f orth from narrow sp ces –F ly
Emerg from darke ss –S hine!
Teach me how to fly!
To g ther nde r y n wing
To nn tn e
To call forth
To send!
Awak n me to third alternati s…
To bt h/And
To ps sib lities
And opr tni ties.
Gie me v sion.
Help m e to see.
Dance me,O Lord of the Dance!

KM

My life has contained the call to priesthood, unnamed, for as long as I remember. I have gone about the work of serving God and leading God's people while an illusive vision shimmered outside the limits of my ability to see. The image would play upon my mind, and I would reach out to grasp it while it receded beyond my touch. I longed for a resolution to the incongruency that persisted, a discontent that convicted me of not living the life that I was chosen to live. I was living out the "next best thing" in countless ways, yet the One Call for which I was born remained unarticulated, unformed in word and name. There was a barrier, a wall, past which I could not see. The music on the other side called to me but I could not get to it. My journals spoke of a butterfly waiting to emerge from a cocoon. I sculpted images of pregnancy and Madonnas with an infant at the breast.

In 20__ I became a member of a group of women who gathered monthly for spiritual discernment over several years. In February, my role was "storyteller," an opportunity to describe an issue for which I sought the movement of the Spirit. I tried to form words that expressed the "disconnect" that I felt. In the course of the silence of one prayer, the illusive vision came into focus for the first time: My call to priesthood. It was like the fog lifted and the wall became transparent. I could see! I could see the Best Thing. I wept. My sisters in faith wept with me. How could I have dreamed this dream when it was unavailable to me? Women are not priests in the Roman Catholic world. How can one imagine the unimaginable? Finding the words and saying them aloud," I am called to priesthood," was obviously a life-changing gift. I am so grateful to the Spirit for revealing Herself to me in the company of my prayer-drenched friends.

From that clarifying moment, the tension accelerated. How could I name this call *and* be a Roman Catholic? Why would my Beloved place this call within my breast only to frustrate me? I prayed, wept, and struggled for weeks.

Early in 21 had enrolled in a work person's Lenten retreat at a spirituality center downtown. One of the features of the retreat was four meetings with a spiritual director. I set up the appointment and looked forward to this experience. When I met Scott, he introduced himself as Father Scott from an independent Catholic church and he was wearing a clerical collar. The quick introduction didn't register with me. I spoke for about forty minutes about being tugged off balance in my life—too much work and not enough play. Finally, I said that I was also trying to figure out what to do with my call to priesthood as a woman in the Roman Catholic Church. I will never forget the look on Scott's face! He asked if I knew who he was. I said, "No." He asked if anyone at the center knew about my call. I responded, "No." He asked if I had requested him for a director and again I said, "No." He asked if I believed in coincidence and once more I said "No." He then said that he was a priest in a Catholic tradition that ordains women! Wow! He wow! God had provided a third alternative to reconcile the separation between woman and priest.

Over the coming months, prayer, research and discussion continued. Shifting to a new expression of my catholicity was not without pain. In the midst of my discernment, I had a vivid dream. In the dream, it was made clear to me that I was "lifting off" in a helicopter toward "home" (interpreted later as priesthood). While hovering I saw young women and girls coming up the stairs from a cellar, into the light. They stood in the bright sunshine squinting and dancing for joy. They had been confined and oppressed in darkness for so long. They exclaimed, "This is what it is to stand in the Light!" The words of the poem at the beginning of my story were given to me, for me and for them. "Dance, O Lord of the Dance!"

As I looked back over my life of then nearly fifty years, the threads had woven a tapestry that I had only seen from the backside, a jumble of knots and lines. I was born the middle child of three daughters in a farming and ranching family in Nebraska. I was baptized and raised in a Roman Catholic home. I received my First Communion and was confirmed when I was seven years of age. We prayed fervently when storms threatened our crops. I remember the "traveling Virgin" coming to our home for a week each year and praying the rosary each evening. The values of family, church, and community were strongly communicated. When I was twelve, I received a diary for Christmas. Reading the entries reveals a girl, a teenager, who was in love with God and eager to serve God to the best of her ability. At that time, I voraciously read books on the lives of the saints. I explored many orders of nuns, seeking a charism that "fit." When I entered high school I participated in youth retreats and activities. I spent time on the farm soaking up the glory of nature in fields, birds, farm animals, wild animals, prairie skies and sunsets. God's presence permeated our senses.

Young adulthood thrust me into self-exploration and occasions for serious decisions. When it was time to choose a college, my dad suggested Regis, believing that a year of philosophy and theology was a foundation that would serve me well. (Thank you, Daddy) I studied sociology along with religious studies; my spirituality began to broaden. I felt a strong call to serve and focused my studies on criminal justice, thinking would serve in corrections. Through a summer internship I came to the realization that lock ing doors and exercising" power over" were not activities that my spirit could tolerate. I began to explore the effects of growing up in an alcoholic family by reading and attending Adult Children of Alcoholic meetings. I engaged in campus ministry, growing close to two Jesuit priests who mentored me.

Greg and I married in September 9 6. I worked for United Way Information and Volunteer Services. The information and referral component of the job exposed me to the breadth and depth of needs of my sisters and brothers and the corresponding service providers, while the volunteer placement side fostered awareness of the rich gifts that generous people had to offer. This job was my first experience in supervising volunteers. Little did I know, it would become the foundation for my entire paid employment career ...and, much later, the life of a pastor.

Meanwhile, Greg and I began to nurture the idea of serving together in the Jesuit Volunteer Corps in the Northwest. The values of justice, community and simple living were appealing. In two we were assigned to be house parents at a girl's group home. The Jesuit influence was remarkable and although the assignment was difficult, the experience changed our lives. No longer could we be carefree, unaware consumers; we had been "ruined for life" by core values that shaped our decisions. Being active in social justice issues and practicing conscientious stewardship of our resources are fundamental approaches to our lives.

The decade of the eighties brought profound changes and challenges and is a "boon" to me. When we returned to Denver after the Corps, I became involved in music and youth ministry at a nearby parish (our home parish of twenty plus years). We purchased a home with space to spare in order to live in community. Our daughter, Mariah was born in and I plunged headlong into motherhood. I stayed at home and relished the earth mother role. Lifelong friendships were formed via a baby sitting coop with local stay at-home moms. Melesa was born in . The first of many housemates in transition or in search of community came to live with us. Greg worked two jobs to support us and I did my best to keep the home front running smoothly.

God called me to prayer in about . I began to read daily Scripture and sit in a "prayer of quiet" (though I did not yet know that this prayer form had a name). I sat in a windowless room (the bathroom!) in the early morning with the door locked, illuminated by a single candle and encountered my Beloved. I fell in love and God's consolation was palpable. I taught aerobics to Christian music! Over time, I was led to participate in the Catholic charismatic movement and was gifted with the grace of praying in the spirit. I studied centering prayer with Father

Thomas Keating at the very beginning of Contemplative Outreach. From Protestant friends, I learned to pray the Word and to stand in faith. I journaled and was given words of poetry. I sculpted in clay and marveled at the spirituality of centering clay on a potter's wheel. It seemed that the hand of God colored every aspect of life.

God trained me by withdrawing Her consolation. For a long period, God seemed absent. My senses were dull and life felt gritty. Persisting in prayer was a trial. I felt abandoned by God, yet was somehow reassured with the agrarian concept of a fallow field. In times of personal crisis, I learned about intercessory prayer for my loved ones. I began to recognize the presence of evil and practiced combat faith. I read and studied voraciously. I became affiliated with a Benedictine abbey nearby, and enjoyed learning about Benedictine spirituality which celebrates the common life and the Daily Office.

Personally, we faced many challenges in the 90s. My paid professional life began in earnest when I went back to working in 90s. I landed a job as a community organizer with Catholic Charities through Metropolitan Organizations for People. I began to learn about power, power of the people. Relationships became paramount and one-to-one visits were the foundation of our work. We worked with member churches and facilitated parish development processes, whereby congregations would identify and develop leaders and faith-based community issues. It was gratifying to help church communities put their faith into action on real life community problems like stop signs and school crossing guards and contaminated water.

At the same time, I began the Master of Arts in Adult Christian Community Development program at Regis College. I remember the thrill of reading the promotional materials. It was a program for parish ministry staff and was "the next best thing" to seminary! We attended summer intensives for three weeks and contracted for independent studies the rest of the year. The summer classes brought wonderful teachers such as theologian John Shea, Kathy Coffey, the Whiteheads, and Avery Dulles. One of my most meaningful and poignant concentrations was the study of grief. Midway through the program, I opted for an emphasis on community leadership which included organizational development and management of financial resources. This path further developed my leadership capacity in developing and shaping new communities of service.

When Catholic Charities decided to develop the SHARE (Self-Help and Resource Exchange) program in Colorado, I applied and transferred to host development. Largely church based, it was a food and community building program. I recruited host organizations and trained their volunteers. This program gave me a platform to publicly speak of the values of community and the affirmation and dignity of each person. In training and personal coaching sessions, I was able to call forth the gifts of a myriad of individuals and set the vision for a wondrous effort. In effect, we developed mini-churches of all faiths, responding to one need to feed each other – literally and figuratively. The statewide staff team of six that I supervised was remarkable. I savored the taste of community, a community that I was privileged to shape. When the director of the program moved on, I stood at the door to directorship and turned away. This program was not the community I was called to lead, but I was gifted with the knowledge that I was called and capable!

In 9? I was involved in a serious car accident. The injuries that I sustained were debilitating and eluded diagnosis for years. The most valuable lessons that I learned through this experience are to recognize my dependence on God, to receive graciously and to value self-care. The accident provided me with St. Paul's "thorn in the side" and I am fully aware that I am one day away from the symptom's reoccurrence. Illusions of being "superwoman" were, thankfully, shattered. And if I didn't embrace the lesson deeply, I was given another opportunity when diagnosed with

Crohn's disease. If I do not take care of myself, pace myself, monitor my workhours, and exercise regularly and deliberately, I find myself incapacitated for a time. This reality combined with the personal experiences of my lifetime form the undergirding for my capacity for compassion, sensitivity to others' pain, ability to be present to others, and deep faith. God is good ...all the time.

Over the years, at our RC parish we led retreats, prepared couples for marriage, and were Eucharistic ministers to the local hospital. I initiated an early morning weekday Communion service and presided and offered "a word" for many years with a group of three to six women who desired a mid-week spiritual touch point. I enjoyed shaping a sacred space, both in the chapel environment and in the life stories shared over the years. On Ash Wednesday, I was privileged to lead a packed chapel in the liturgy of the word, the ancient ritual of imposition of ashes and distribution of communion. It would be the closest I could come to ordained ministry and it filled me with a sense of being where I was called to be. I was privileged to journey with three adults as their sponsor through RCIA (Rite of Christian Initiation of Adults). I gathered our small faith community in weekly prayer and study for the seasons of Advent and Lent. We also celebrated sacramental moments such as births, deaths, rites of passage such as going away to college. Greg and I were chaperones and leaders for World Youth Day in Denver in 9? and accompanied a group of thirty-five youth pilgrims, including our daughters, to Paris in 9?. I have delighted in making our home sacramental, creating rituals and traditions that recognize the spiritual and religious aspects in our everyday lives. We especially appreciate and have found meaning in the passing of our blessing upon special occasions.

In 9? began to record the daily Mass lectionary reading for my grandma who suffered macular degeneration. It grew to a subscription base maximum of about ?? subscribers per month, the majority of whom are blind or visually impaired. I include a "thoughts for the day," created by sitting with the Word and studying resources, endeavoring to bring Scripture to the life of my subscribers. This service is time intensive, a labor of love. I am gratified by the supportive notes that we receive from nuns in infirmaries, priests who are enabled (through this service) to offer daily Mass, and sighted individuals who listen to the Word on their way to work each day. This ministry reached out to, in retrospect, my first congregation – one hundred-plus people hearing my voice every day.

My work prior to and after SHARE involved the recognizing of people's gifts, calling them forth and directing them toward a common vision, on a foundation of faith. I have learned about shaping conflict constructively and believe my leadership experiences have prepared me for parish leadership. I recently asked my mother if she had seen "the priest" in me. She said "Of course! You were always 'that way.'" I have always led on extended family prayer, written notes of encouragement and acted as the peacemaker, moving toward reconciliation. Others have seen "the priest" in me as well. David Moore, the director of SHARE Colorado at the time, repeatedly asked me why I continued to live "beneath my potential." He saw my leadership and spiritual qualities and called me to stand "higher." When he was afflicted with an inoperable brain tumor, he called me to help him develop a video testimony to his life for his wife and daughters and to create a healing service for him. Seated at the table with his parish priest and music minister, I was graced with a flash of "my potential." The service was wonderfully sacramental: celebrating the gift of David in our lives and calling forth healing at every level. As it turned out, although healing was witnessed at many levels, David's physical healing was not granted. I was asked to write and give the eulogy at his funeral.

I have a gift for expressing our faith in symbol and sign, word and music. I was privileged to write and give the eulogies at the funerals of my grandfather, uncles and aunts. I wrote ecumenical prayer-liturgies for coworkers at the City of Northglenn following the tragedies of Columbine and September 11th. Even in a city government environment, people need to gather and remember Who holds us together. I wrote and led a memorial prayer service for Greg's family when his grandfather died. I chose the readings and wrote the prayers of the faithful for the funeral Mass of Greg's sister.

A year prior to the naming of my priestly call, I was moved to work on "finding my Voice" and to stand in my truth in a more overt manner. I decided to begin to develop retreats. I have since offered three retreats, including a two-day Lenten retreat entitled "Celebrating the Cross" for a sister church community. My pastors also encouraged me to prepare for my ordination as deacon by preparing and offering homilies. Slowly, but surely, I gained confidence in the legitimacy of my preparation for this vocation, via formal and informal education and depth of experience. I was coming out of the darkness into the light.

My life is blessed and rich. My husband is my life partner and is involved directly or as support in everything I do, in everything I am. He is my "Jesus with skin on" who mirrors my divine image back to me. He is a man of God. Our grown children are delightful women who teach me about true appreciation of diversity they live what we taught them! We have wonderful friends with whom we have shared mutual support for nearly forty years. Who could ask for more?

There are moments in my life when I know I am in the right place at the right time. Most of these moments are pastoral in nature: Proclaiming the Word, sitting at the bedside of a hospitalized person offering Communion and listening attentively, writing liturgies that are expressive of our deep held faith and rich humanity, leading the gathered in song and prayer, holding the Christ Light for someone in crisis, facilitating a group in a visioning or planning exercise, rocking on a glider and sons, laying on my husband's shoulder as we drift off to sleep..and in these moments I am blessed with peace. The most profoundly spiritual experience of my life was holding on the emaciated two pound, thirteen ounce grandson, Aiden, nearly every day for three months while he was hospitalized fighting for his life in 2003. I learned discipline when overcoming the fatigue of my ordinary responsibilities and commitments in order to drive to the hospital. I learned to "float on a river of grace" that sustained me day after day. I learned not to count the cost, and that I would be given the strength to do the work I was called to do. I saw Jesus in Aiden's eyes, the Jesus of the Least of These, fixing his gaze on me, and I was blessed.

All the days of my life prepared me to stand fully in my call to priesthood. The years that followed were a whirlwind of exhilarating new experience and transcripts, additional study, preparation for the transitional diaconate, and finally to be ordained a priest on July 2011. And along the way, to collaborate with a priest colleague and mentor to form a community of faith, Church of the Beloved Ecumenical Catholic Community.

Now, a dozen years into being priest and pastor, I truly float on a river of grace. I live with the privilege of serving God's people as priest. I delight in celebrating Mass, training liturgical ministers, visiting the sick, baptizing babies (my grandsons included), sitting with the dying, forming a parish council, and preaching. Our community has wonderful souls who are growing in love and teaching me how to love.

All those years ago, sculpting figures of Mary, this is the message she gave to me for serving as priest:

> There is no one outside of grace. The whole world is held
> in the embrace of God, our Mother and Father. When
> they come, as they will, hungry, tired and poor, feed them.
> Have you heard of Stone Soup? Set a banquet before
> them. Rest them. Shepherds find green grass to relax upon

*– give them space to set their burdens down. Heal them –
anoint them with oil, honor them, bind up their wounds.
Tell them stories – let them know about the kindom of
God. Move among them. Love them. Pour out your love
in abundance.*

This is the priest I aspire to be. I have emerged gloriously
from the cocoon in which I was formed and am dancing with the
Spirit. I am grateful to be enabled to live life out of call, to do
and be "the Best Thing

THIS JOURNEY OF AWAKENING

Mary Ramerman

W hat is a calling? What does it mean when someone ask me how I was called to the p iesthood? Was there a moment when I wok p nd heard that oi ce clearlyw ithin me? Or did it come slowly ik the fog olling n oe r Penob cot Bayf or see ral hon s b fore one realizes one is immersed in it?

When I look back I find my pull to the priesthood came as earlya s my see nth y ar,w hen I dip d myt oe into the g eat rie r of life and felt its tb lingn e in. There has b en mu h to learn ab ti the cn rent of this waterwaya s it winds its way through the open fields and craggy gorges of my lifetime. There hae b en times to swim hard and times to let the water carry me. There were longp riods of leai ng he rie r b hind and choosing the p e d road along ts b nk . Sometimes all I coli d do was watch it sp rk e and dance as I lays till pn i ts g ant bli ders. Ultimately,i t has b en a p ocess of discoe ringhow to b one with the force of the river, flowing with it in its lazy pools and gasping for air in its rushing rapids. The force of the river is not the water; it is what moves the water. Without the power stirring it, the water is stagnant. In me, it is the same. The power within me awakens my soul to move with all of creation. The moment of discovering my call was not one, but many moments together leading to an awareness of whom I am called to be. I do not think this journey of awakening is over. My understanding of how I am part of this river of life will continue to expand like the view from a spaceship pulling away from Earth, showing the planet in an infinitely greater context. At any point in time I am there at both the apex of my calling and at the beginning of it. My calling provides the theme of my life: the setting, the focus, the knowledge, and the perspective. For another, the calling may be to medicine or teaching or engineering or art. For me, it is ministry and within that, the priesthood. It is with this understanding that I hope by present these moments in my life of being called to the priesthood.

Sadie Wilson was the oldest member of the Sonoma Methodist Church. She was almost ninety years old. She wore black high-top shoes with long laces and dresses that came down to her calves. Sometimes she had a lace shawl around her shoulder that used to be white but was now more the color of tea. Her white hair made a bun at the back of her head and her face was covered with wrinkles. She taught the second grade Sunday school class. Every Sunday morning seven of us children went to her classroom and sat around the rectangular wooden table. There were pictures of Jesus on the wall. She would tell us a Bible story and then give us a verse to memorize. When we came back the next week we had to repeat the verse and cite the book and chapter that it came from. I liked the challenge Sadie gave us every week, though I had no idea how valuable those verses would be in my future.

Sunday was a favorite morning for me. Getting to church on time was a chaotic process. All six of us Whitfield children had to wake, have breakfast, and get dressed in Sunday clothes. For the four girls this meant a dress, black patent leather shoes, socks with lace on them, and white gloves. The boys had pressed pants and ties. We were piled into the station wagon with the brown wooden sides, being careful to stay out of the way of my father's hand. He was quick to slap a slow-moving child. Once we got to church, we filed into a pew where we would spend the next hour listening to a half-hour sermon and singing old people's songs from the Methodist hymnal. My sister and I would take the offertory envelope out of its wooden holder and use the small pencil to play Hangman during the sermon. My father, one of Sonoma's few family physicians, would often get paged during the service. He would leave and go to the Sonoma Valley Hospital and come back for us later. My mother was always deeply moved during the service at which point the message would be whispered from child to child, "Mom's crying again."

After the service the Methodists always had a coffee hour. This was the best part. Two white-haired ladies would sit at the end of a long table covered with white linens. Silver coffee pots were located at each end, and they would pour a cup of coffee for the adults. In the middle were all kinds of plates with cookies and coffee cakes on them. We would slip in to grab a piece of cake and then take off running through the building. We knew every nook and cranny of the Methodist church. We were allowed full access to every room except the Pastor's office, which was always locked. When we reached the age of thirteen and were confirmed, we were even given a key to the building. We utilized these keys in high school when we would slip out of our classrooms and walk down seven blocks to the church. I had two keys on my keychain, one to our kitchen door at home and one to the kitchen door at church.

On the best Sundays, my father would take all of us to Vella's Ice Cream Parlor on the corner of the plaza. We would each get a chocolate milkshake, which came in a tall fluted glass. The milkshake that didn't fit in the glass came alongside in the metal container it was mixed in. We sat on the barstools at the counter, twisting from side to side, sipping those shakes. It was heaven!

All of this laid the foundation for me to fall in love with Jesus. During the day I talked to him constantly. He was my companion, guiding me, loving me, and speaking to me often through the verses I had memorized his words coming back to me as different situations required his advice. At night he stayed with me on a prayer card tacked on my wooden bulb-d, where he was pictured knocking on a wooden door with a glow-in-the-dark cross above it. I knew he was there with me.

Life was stressful for me at home. My father was a dedicated doctor to his patients but a volatile father and husband at home. My mother devoted her life to keeping quiet and out of the way of his temper. I became a quiet girl spending hours reading in my room, doing well in school, and avoiding anything that might draw his anger. My talks with Jesus were frequent. He and I would sit together seated on a grass-covered hill. Sometimes he would hold my hand as we walked along a little stream. He was always there for me to go to, and his loving presence and messages were powerfully clear to me.

It was in those early years that I knew I would become a Methodist minister. Even when my parents stopped going to church, I continued to go, getting a ride from my girlfriends who also attended church there. In junior high I babysat the little children in the nursery. In high school I attended the youth group in the new building with the fireplace and couches. I became a youth representative for the California-Nevada Methodist Conference and began to travel around the state to meetings and retreats. Those events took me out of the little town of Sonoma to the diverse cities of San Francisco and Oakland and Stockton. I met Black and Hispanic youth, liberal college students, and people passionate about social justice issues and politics. My own opinions about life were beginning to form, and I saw myself as part reformer/part missionary. I would be an advocate for the poor, I would develop my own skills so I could help them, and I would live my life connected to them.

It was in my junior year of high school that I saw a poster advertising a summer job as a camp counselor. It was an outdoor live-in camp and paid $50 per week. I applied and went to my interview with, to my surprise, a Catholic priest. He later told me how surprised *he* was to have this quiet young Methodist girl apply, but he was intrigued by my calling to ministry and hired me anyway. My first two weeks were tough for me as most of the counselors knew each other from Catholic school, and I felt alone. But I loved sleeping under the stars, Mass in the outdoor chapel, and the experience of backpacking through the mountains, swimming in the river and horseback riding with our young campers. I bonded with the young women I met there, and we were inseparable friends through college. One summer another counselor and I rebelled against the backpacking imitations that were set for girls, and took a group of teen girls through the mountains all the way to the Pacific Ocean. For the next ten years, I would spend my summers at Camp St. Michael, eventually becoming the Camp Program Director and administrator. It was there that I first experienced a Catholic Mass. I walked away from it reflecting on the extraordinary sermon I had just heard. I was surprised at the next Mass to hear exactly the same sermon again. It was then that I discovered that what I thought was the sermon were the Eucharistic prayers. My experience with the Catholic Church had begun.

It was in college that I met Jim Ramerman. He was music major at Humboldt State University and a gregarious, fun loving man who swept me off my feet. He lived in a Catholic commune—five youth ministers who worked with a Catholic priest leading youth groups around Humboldt County. Many of my counselor friends were part of this CYO organization. I began to attend the meetings and retreats with Jim. Before long I was leading wo yth g op on myow n. The p iest was committed to trainings in all thing haiv ng o do with g opp ocess and commni cation sk lls and theolog . We sp nt on week nds in an ab ndoned rectory n Fortna that we reestab ished as a retreat center. We were either leadingyth h retreats for teens in Hm - bl dt Cont y,or attending rainings essions on selv s. We traveled as a team to the LA CCD Cong ess and b g n org nizing statewide ev nts for yth h ministers.

~

  Jim and I married just a month after my twenty-first birthday. The weddingc eremonyw as mu h more impr tant to me than the recep ion. We chose the theme of All Good Gifts from the ms i- cal "Godsp ll." The b atu ifu old St.B ernard's chn ch in En e- ka, CA was filled with friends and symbols of our lives together. There were artistic b nners dep cting B rother Sn a nd Sister Moon. A small redwood tree g aced the altar. The ms ic þ ay d ym yb other George and sister Elaine spk to God's p esence in on liv s and in on friends. A teacher of mys ister Carol,S wa- mi Day nanda,w ho hap ned to b sp ak ng hat weeka t Hm - bl dt State Univ rsity, a ttended on wedding. He was dressed in the traditional orang rob s of a holym an from India,a nd his p esence was hard to miss. The recep ion was held in the chn ch hall,þ on yf riends who sp nt hon s mak ngs andwiches and decoratingf or u . All of these small details were syn bl s of the life ahead of u ,f rom the simþ e liv ngc hoices to the b oadening of on relig ou p rsp ctiv to inclde the wisdom of other faiths. We didn't kow it y t,b thing were soon to chang dramati- cally.

  For the next six years, we continued our education and began our careers. Both Jim and I became teachers and then shifted our focus to ministry. I became a Catholic. Together, we earned our Master's degrees in Theology from St. Mary's College in Moraga, CA. We began working for the Diocese of

Santa Rosa, rnni ngp og ams for ytu h ministry,C YO,a nd the
sm mer camp. While the workw as exciting he diocese was not.
It became the center of scandals in sexual abuse and financial
mismanag ment. We were g owing ncreasing ydi sillu ioned
with the chn ch in which we were work nga nd b g n to search
for an alternativ mission for on liv s.

We annonc ed to the Diocese that we wolu d b leaiv nga t the
end of the school y ar. We focu ed on creatinga new þ an for
on selv s and attended a discernment retreat for that p ps e. At
the retreat, we were told to take our Bibles and find a quiet place
otu side to sit. We were asked to find a passage and then imagine
on selv s in that p ssag ,p ctn ingon selv s as p rt of the story.
I fond a shadys pt nde r a tree and op ned myB ib e to Mark
the storyof the rich yngm an. I read the p ssag ,c losed my
ey s,a nd instantlyf elt my elf transpr ted to a g opf p ob e
g thered arond J esu .

*Jesus was speaking to all of us. He caught my eye and I
asked him, "Jesus, can I go with you?" "Yes," he said without
hesitation. "Oh, but Jesus, I can't go with you," I said. "You see,
I have a little baby and it's very hard to travel with a baby." I
began to tell him all about my one-year-old Matthew and all the
baby equipment I had to take with me. He said, "Wherever I go,
Matthew can go, too." And then Jesus and I were walking together and Matthew was walking along with us running from side to
side. When Jesus began to speak to the group again, Matthew
was making noise. "You see, Jesus," I said, "He wants to run all
over the place." "Let him run," said Jesus, "and you will still be
able to hear everything I say." So I let Matthew run in the field,
and as I ran after him I could still hear Jesus' voice speaking to
the group.*

*Then I was back under the tree again listening to Jesus speak
to the group. Again, he looked at me, and again I said, "Jesus,
can I go with you?" "Yes," he replied. "Oh but I can't. You see,*

*I'm married to Jim, and I don't know if Jim wants to go too."
Jesus said, "You can come with me and still be with Jim."*

And then, a third time, I was under the tree again listening to Jesus speak to the group. For the third time, I said, "Jesus, can I go with you?" And for the third time, he replied, "Yes." "Oh, but I can't go. You see, we just bought a house. And when you buy a house you have to live in it for a few years before you sell it or you will lose money." And I began to tell Jesus everything I knew about buying a house.

But then the meditation ended. I was back in Santa Rosa at the retreat. I tried hard to close my eyes and return to my visit with Jesus, but I could not.

I returned inside to the group that was waiting for me. People shared their experiences. When it came time to share mine, everyone listened intently. The leader of the retreat said to me, "Mary, you need to write this down. It is a gift, and it will grow in meaning for you." He was right. It did grow in meaning for me. We sold our home a few months later and began our move across the continent to Rochester, New York. We packed our camping gear in our Volkswagen Rabbit, shipped a few boxes of personal belongings and toys, and headed East with our two-year-old son, Matthew.

Our move brought us from sunny California to Rochester with long winters and humid summers. We left our redwoods and ocean beaches for an inner city environment with city parks. We sold our new home and moved into a two-family home where one-half of the structure had been donated to the parish. Everything in the home was painted green, including all the kitchen cabinets and the furniture. The windows were covered with plastic sheeting to keep out the blinds, and the wooden floor was covered with years of wax and grime. The parish had promised to take care of all of our needs, but it was quickly apparent that the priest in charge had not thought about such things as a vacuum cleaner, dressers, or kitchen utensils. If we waited awhile, he assured us, someone would donate a car we could use and a better bed. After a few months, someone did donate a used washer and dryer that blew up after we had spent a Saturday maneuvering it into the tiny basement. At that point a generous woman in the parish gave us a band new washer and dryer, sparking some hope in me that maybe this would work out after all. I was determined to "live simply" and devote ourselves to this new mission that God had for us. If that meant living on a small salary of $$ or on family, joining a co-op of food, and getting by with donated furniture and clothing was fine for it. I hadn't yet discovered that living without enough could be as distracting as living with too much.

The first six months in Rochester were cold and lonely. A group of parishioners at Corpus Christi were upset that outsiders had been hired. They wanted us to go away. I missed my home in California, where I had spent the first twenty-eight years of my life. I wondered why we were there.

In February I traveled on a parish trip to Port-au-Prince, Haiti. We stayed at a simple hostel run by a group of nuns. During the day we took a trip to work at one of Mother Teresa's homes for young girls dying of tuberculosis. I went from bed to bed, singing songs in French and massaging their dry skin with lotion. The minutes went by so slowly. I panicked at one point, thinking my group had gone and left me behind. I asked one of the sisters how she did this work day after day. She replied, "There is only one way to do this work. And that is to pray. We pray three hours a day, in the morning, at lunch, and in the evening. Without prayer, we could not do it." Her words made me realize how little I was doing. It was clear that I did not need to pray as much because I was not giving enough of myself to require it. I left determined to both pray more and do more for God.

Another trip took us to the poorest slums outside the city. When we arrived we saw a long line of people waiting outside a clinic. One woman spotted me. She left her spot at the front of

the line, and came over to me carrying a small baby. She handed
me the baby and asked, "Will you take my baby with you?" I
was shocked and replied, "The baby loves you not me." She
responded, "The baby is hungry and I can't feed it." I can still
feel her eyes upon me and hear the flatness in her voice. I did not
physically take her baby home with me. But I have carried her
in my heart ever since and thanked her for the moment I realized
that I am not just a mother for my own child, but for every child
on this planet.

During my first few years at Corpus Christi, my brother
George would often drive from Virginia to visit me. He would
bring his partner, Tom, and we would have fun just sitting on
the front porch and telling stories. Tom's family had owned a
farm in Virginia for generations, and now it was in Tom's capable
hands. One time they told me how on Sunday they had gone to
Tom's Baptist church in the local town. Posted on the door that
day was a handwritten sign, "No queers allowed." I promised
them both that I would never have a church that turned gay people away. In the 80s there were many people dying of AIDS.
Many churches turned them away and refused to celebrate their
funerals. At Corpus we celebrated many of their funerals, and we
came to know many people in the gay community. One organist,
who was also gay, told us, "We don't want to just die from here.
We want to live from here, too." That began our ministry to the
gay and lesbian community and eventually to the LGBTQ+ people who are a core part of our parish.

Corpus Christi continued on a path of opening outreaches to
those who were poor or disenfranchised. As we welcomed the
homeless, the imprisoned, the children, the naked, and the dying
on little 8s came alive with joy and passion. I was invited to
preach at the Masses, along with other lay women and men who
had real life experience to share. I loved connecting the scriptures to the day-to-day adventures happening in our outreaches
and in my growing family. I loved giving, studying the scriptures,

finding stories that related, and constructing a homily. I also loved knowing the people sitting in the pews and serving them. My role at Corpus Christi was growing into the position of Associate Pastor.

In ____ the liturgy committee suggested that I wear a white alb when I was on the altar during a service. We purchased one that came with a colorful white banner that hung down from the left shoulder. They liked the idea that I could coordinate this with the color of the priest's stole. Before I could wear it at Corpus, my brother George died suddenly at the age of ___ from pneumonia. The first time I wore the alb was to celebrate his funeral. After that, I wore it for every Mass.

In ____ the earth shook under the foundation of Corpus Christi when Cardinal Ratzinger, then Prefect of the Congregation for the Doctrine of the Faith, wrote a letter to Bishop Clark asking him to remove Fr. Jim Callan from Corpus Christi. There were three reasons given for his dismissal: the prominent role of women on the altar, the marrying of gay and lesbian couples, and the welcoming of everyone to the Eucharist. This event impacted the communities of Corpus Christi and Rochester in many powerful ways. For me, it began a time of leadership of a radical community willing to forego the inclusion of people who had come to value and love their Catholic Masses. With Fr. Jim sent away to exile in Elmira, the congregation looked to me for leadership and support. They were a powerful force, with lay leaders coming from every possible profession ready to help save their church and its ministries. They organized protest marches through the city of Rochester, demonstrations in front of the Diocesan Chancery, and PR packets to be distributed to national news media including Time Magazine, the New York Times, and CBS News. Two women were assigned from the diocese to run Corpus Christi. I held the belief that we could work these differences out and Corpus Christi could continue to thrive. A friend, a seasoned businessman, cautioned me, " Mary, this is a corporate shake down. I've been through this before, and I can tell you there is nothing that you can do to stop it."

In the end, I discovered he was right. By the end of 9 most of the staff had been let go, a new priest was in place, and many people had left Corpus. But new life had already begun in the weekly gathering that we had on Tuesday nights at the Downtown Presbyterian Church. Now I found myself the celebrant of the services, inviting guest preachers and offering a communion service where all of the people participated in the words of consecration. It was a passionate, creative time with an unknown future ahead of us.

I was fired from Corpus Christi on October 15. It was the feast day of St. Teresa of Avila, the sixteenth-century Spanish mystic and church reformer. I was told I could keep my job if I never preached again and never set foot on the altar. I would be expected to come to Mass and sit in the pews. I asked the two women firing me what message that would that give to the congregation, if their woman minister was not allowed to go near the altar? I refused to abide by such a discriminatory lie, and was fired. They gave me until the next day at noon to clean out my office of fifteen years. The boxes I took home would remain unopened in my basement for another fifteen years.

The discrimination and injustice in the Catholic Church became visible to me. It was as though I had received a new pair of glasses and everything around me had suddenly come into focus. For years I had benefited from working with a progressive priest in an inner city congregation. I had the freedom to preach, to lead the opening prayer at Mass, to lift the cup during the consecration, and to participate in weddings. At the request of women who had suffered abuse from men, I had heard their confessions at our reconciliation services. People could choose to come to one of the priests present, or to come to a corner and speak to their woman minister. My line of people was the longest in the church, a testament to the percentage of women who have suffered abuse from men in their liv s. All of this evl v d ov r time in a natu al and spr tiv way. It was a shockf or me to discov r that many women servinga s p storal associates did not hav the freedom to minister in these way or the freedoms theydi d hav had b en tak n awayi n the last few y ars. Myc owork r,(now Rev.) My a Brown,de scrib d it to me in this way," Mary,yu v b en the favr ed slav in the Master's Hon e. You v had plentyt o eat and a nice þ ace to sp nd yn day. That's whyyu v new r thoþt ab tu reb llingor leav ng he þ antation.B tu all the time you've had the good life, your sisters out in the fields have been sfi ferinğ

It was an ex raordinaryt ime for me. There was a serv ce to þ an each week. Memb rs of the chn ch were meetingda ilyt o þ an their nex p otest. The p ess was constantlyc alling o inter- iv ew me abtu the scandal of on reb llion ag inst the Catholic Chn ch that was tak nþ ace at Corp . Goingotu in þ ic was worrisome,a s manyp oþ e wolu d stop me to either ex ess their ap eciation for standingf or women or chastise me for at- tack ng he Catholic Chn ch. Myt hree children were sfi feringa s their teachers offered their jdn ents abtu me to their classes. Ev n myhn b nd fond hi s leadership coachees wanted to talk abtu his wife and what was hap ning at "that Catholic chn ch." Sometimes I sat in a rock ngc hair in on liv ng oom,l ook ng otu at the increasing yc hillyl andscap ,w onderingv hat I wolu d do for the rest of myl ife.

On one particular down day, I flipped on the news to see the story of Matthew Shephard, a young gay man in Wyoming who had been brutally beaten and left hanging on a fence post to die. The churches were eerily silent on his horrific murder. I was overcome with the awareness that as a minister I had to speak out on behalf of gays and lesbians. I realized that I had to stop feeling hurt by these small nasty comments, and instead have the courage to speak out for those who are truly marginalized. If I didn't have the guts to do that, then what was the point of following Jesus? Matthew Shepherd became an inspiration for me, a spirit guide leading me through the maze of criticism and rejection that would follow in the months ahead.

On February 15, 1999, we held our first services as a new inclusive Catholic Church. Salem United Church of Christ welcomed us in their sanctuary. There were about a thousand of us "roamin' Catholics," as the news media called us. We were no longer welcome on any property belonging to the Diocese of Rochester. The news reports informed us we had "excommunicated" ourselves. But instead of a dreary, hopeless end to our community, we were on fire with a desire to reignite the spirit in our church. After six months we did two major things: We chose the name Spiritus Christi, thus moving from the body of Christ to the spirit of Christ, and we opened our first outreach, the Grace of God Recovery House for men. It was significant and deliberate to make our first investment in a home for the poor rather than in a church building for ourselves. We also welcomed LGBTQ members to fully participate in our community, offering them participation in all the sacraments including marriage. We welcomed everyone to come to Jesus' table for communion. The question remaining on the table was how to ordain a woman priest.

In the next three years, a group of forty of the faithful ly met with me every month to discern a path for ordination. We hosted a Women's Ordination Conference in and invited women from around the world to come. It was there that I met leaders in the worldwide movement, including Elfriede Harth from France, Sr. Maureen Fiedler from the US, and (now Bishop) Christine Mayr-Lumetzberger from Austria. Rev. Suzanne Hiatt, one of the original Philadelphia Eleven ordained women Episcopal priests, came and shared how difficult her journey had been. At the end of the conference she spoke again, saying how she had expected to find women idealizing the path to priesthood, and instead was pleased to find courageous and strong women ready for the battle ahead. After the conference we were determined to meet ag in, b only for an ordination, not another meeting

On g ou now accomp nied by women from arond t he world, c onsidered many w ays to g t me ordained. These inclde d finding a bishop on his deathbed that, with his last dying breath, woli d b eak with tradition and raise his arm to ordain a woman. No su h thing ha p ned. We ep ored ordination in the Ep sco- p l tradition, b fond I woli d hav to mov six m iles away from my c hn ch and family f or sev ral y ars to accomb ish that. We considered simb y de claring m e ordained Ṣ p rit Christi, b we wanted a ceremony hat woli d b credib e to the wider Catholic pp li ation. We were sn e that k nd of credib lit y e- q red a b shop h whom?

In 0 ask d the g op o tak three months off from meeting a nd dev t e on time to p ay r. I went on a retreat to Palm Desert, C alifornia with a woman that I had recently m et at a conference in San Dieg. R ev. K athy M cCarthy old me she had b en ordained B ishop P eter Hick an, a nd inv ted me to come to their retreat. I joined the small g op of eit p iests and Bishop P eter for a day of p ay r and discn sion. We met in a small condo owned by one of the p iests. The sn rondi ng were simb e, b the dep h of the p op e p esent was p ofond . I ke w that day hat I had fond m y t rib . (Years later, B ishop H ick man's commni tw oli d g ow to inclde hndr eds of men and women p iests.)

A few months later, B ishop Peter Hick an came to Sp rit Christi to meet on commni ty. Two hndr ed p op e tn ned on to interv ew this Bishop a nd see if he was the rit p rson to ordain n . (At this pi nt, a nother woman on on staff, (now Rev) Denise Donato, was finishing her theology degree and was also interested in ordination.) He was ask d many q stions inclld ng whether or not the women p iests ordained woli d hav to lead a celib te life. When he rep ied "no," my hn b nd, J im, s tood pi n the middle of the cong eg tion and clap d enth iastically.

We had found our bishop. Now we began the planning of the ordination. Where would we have it? Fr. Jim Callan and I went to a large and historical venue on Main Street in Rochester, the Eastman Theater. We asked for December 8th. The woman behind the desk simply laughed. "We book several years in advance," she said. We asked her to look around that date and she began digging and agreed to do so." Well," she said," I'm amazed to find this, but the morning of November 17 is open." That was it!

The ordination planning was underway. There were committees for the decorations, the music, the liturgical dancers, the children and banners, the Eucharistic ministers, the luncheon following the ordination, speakers, public relations, and security. Two nights before the ordination, every room in the church was filled with people rehearsing and meeting about the coming event.

The day of my ordination was an unseasonably warm and sunny November day in Rochester. In my yard a bush of yellow roses, planted after my brother George's death, was in full bloom. The night sky would be in a shower of shooting stars described by CNN in this way *"One of the best meteor showers in decades barraged the planet before dawn Sunday, raining down thousands of streaking points of light each hour during its peak."*

I waited outside in the hallway while the Eastman Theatre filled to its capacity of 3000 people. While I knew many of the people there, others whom I had never met had traveled hundreds of miles to attend the ordination of a woman they didn't know. Over the years to come, I would meet them one by one in various parts of the country and they would tell me," I was there at your ordination." When I asked why they came, the depth of the meaning that a woman's ordination held for them poured out, including how it verified for them the authenticity of their own relationship with God.

As I entered the hall following he p rade of children and litn g cal dancers,m inisters and p iests,i t was if I were in another realm. It was a divine place, one overflowing with love and spr t and joy. The ms ic of the choirs and the b atingof the drm set the stag for what was coming.. *Siyahamba, We are Marching in the Light of God.*

The ceremony for entering the priesthood is filled with sm bl ism. At one pi nt I laya t the foot of the cross while the cong eg tion sanga Litanyof the Saints. I laym he ad on a p llow emb oidered for me M an een Nielsen,a yngv oman who was devt inge r life to caringf or orpa ns in Haiti when a man wantinghe r small amont of cash shot her pi ntb anlS he had died js t eibt months p ior to myor dination. Her p esence filled my heart.

At another pi nt myde ar friend and cowork r,M imi Yong man,p aced the chasb e ov r myhe ad. As she did it felt as if a ki fe had slashed a rop from arond m yne ck..t he rop that had b en drag nga hg weibt b hind me.I was sdde nly free to float up into the air. I was free of the b den of hav ng o minister withou the credib lityof a title or ps ition. I was free to claim myow n calling hat had b en in me for forty two y ars. I was free and readyt o b a p iest.

THE UNEQUIVOCAL YES

Rosean Mae Amaral

"In order to discern we need to learn how to read on own history, to see the tn ning pi nts, the mov ments of chang , the nf olding of God's plan for ɴ at each new step of the way." Esther de Waal, *Seeking God: The Way of St. Benedict*

It's a simp e story,r eally— nd an amazing one .O n Vicar deliv red an awesome homily hat Snda y n late Sep emb r, She op ned ps crip n e in a way hat took he lid off the bxv here God is held hostag . I coli dn't wait to talk ith her after Mass to see if we coli d meet for coffee and sp nd some time np cking hat Gosp l messag a b t fn ther.E x itedly ap oaching her,I thank d the Vicar for her words and ask d, "Could we go for coffee so I could find out what the process is for b coming a deacon?" She ask d," You ant to kow abu b coming a deacon?" It was only pn he r clarify ng m y eq st that I realized what I had said. So I replied, "I guess so!" We set a time and place to meet in November, since the Synod was in October, and on clergy and delegates were preparing for this gathering. Before I could meet with the Vicar, the delegates from my parish, Mary of Magdala Ecumenical Catholic Community, returned from Synod. I was approached by a few delegates who said they had witnessed the ordination of three women to the Diaconate at Synod, and they asked me if I would be the Deacon for our faith community. I remember standing before them crying and saying, "I already have an appointment with the Vicar to discuss this ministry. I am so moved that you have called me too."

I felt twice blessed, and twice called.

In November I met with the Vicar and learned what would be needed from me if I wished to continue toward the Diaconate. First, I would need to send in a letter of intent. Yet, for me, the pendulum of uncertainty was still swinging. I remembered the words of a cherished spiritual director saying, "Do not make a decision if the pendulum is still swinging. Keep on discerning." So I did.

Why me, God? Now, at age 68? I felt a kindred spirit with Sarah when she was told she would have a child in her advanced years. Was it really you, God, calling me? I was unsure, like the young Samuel who continued to run to Eli saying, "Here I am. You called me." Seriously, God, the only thing I have in common with Moses is the white hair, so how can I lead your people? But I remained in discernment and prayer each day.

One of my most steadfast spiritual practices is *lectio divina*. Each morning I awake at 6 AM, read the Old Testament, Psalms, and the New Testament, and then choose one word or phrase that moves me that day and I write a short reflection. I have been doing this for fifteen years. This practice has guided many of my life decisions, and I hoped it would continue to reveal God's will for me. In the meantime, I was getting pretty and on about that pendulum swinging back and forth, back and forth. Nothing definite yet. This gave me plenty of time to doubt: I am not worthy of this call, and how can I be sure it is really God who is calling? I also had lots of time to ponder: I'm a woman, and how long have I prayed for women clergy in the Catholic church? Why is there a felt sense in every cell of my body calling me to seek and serve God in all people? Back and forth, back and forth.

At this time I was truly blessed to have a discernment team that followed the process informed by the Diaconal Formation Committee of our Church. They were always questioning, always clarifying, always loving, and always directing me to stay focused on the voice of God and God's will for me. The days passed and we entered the month of December, 2014.

In our Catholic tradition the Feast of the Annunciation falls on the 25th of March. It is the remembrance of the angel Gabriel being sent from God to Mary of Nazareth with the Good News that she had found favor with God and would conceive in her womb and give birth to Jesus, the son of God. We all know this story, the part. I was working so hard to get to that Yes! That unequivocal Yes! of our Blessed Mother. I thought that maybe by March 25th I would know for sure that this call was true.

But it was only December 4th, and I was so frustrated with pendulum swinging and ranted to my partner, Lannie, "If God wants me to be a Deacon then why doesn't God send me an angel? Mary got an angel who was straight forward in delivering God's message, why can't I? Lannie was scared, very scared and said "Watch out what you wish for." I ignored her warning and retorted, "The angel's message would be clear, 'God wants you to be a deacon.'" Then, truly knowing I would continue with the program of study, background check, psychological testing providing answers to deep spiritual questions, being mentored by one of our Ecumenical Catholic priests, remaining in spiritual direction, being interviewed by priests, deacons and finally, the

9

presiding bishop and moving it along to prepare ring for ordination. Easy, huh? But the pendulum was still swinging. DRAT!

On the eighth day of the month I awoke at 6 AM, on the Feast Day of the Immaculate Conception. The Gospel reading was The Annunciation. I faithfully read the passage and wrote my daily reflection. Four days later on December 12th, The Feast Day of Our Lady of Guadalupe, the Gospel reading was The Annunciation. I faithfully read the passage and wrote my daily reflection. On December 20th, the Gospel reading was The Annunciation. I faithfully read the passage and wrote my daily reflection. Finally, on December 21st, I sat in bed at 6 A.M., opened my Bible, and amazingly, the Gospel reading was The Annunciation, for the fourth time in the month of December,

The angel I had asked for had arrived.

The Holy Ones did not wait until March 8th to call on me. They called on me in December of . The angel Gabriel had been sent from God to a town named Fort Collins, to a 6 year-old woman in a committed life-long relationship with her partner Laurie, and the woman's name was Rosean. "Hail, favored one! The Lord is with you." This is what I heard as I read the Annunciation for the fourth time, and my heart cried out "YES! OH, YES! May it be done to me according to your Word." The pendulum stopped dead in its tracks. I had truly been called by God!

For the next three days my "Yes!" written on a small piece of paper, sat on my home altar. I wanted God to see my final answer, and I also wanted to make sure the pendulum would not start swinging. It did not. Instead, I felt the peace that comes from knowing that my discernment was complete and true.

And so it was that after much study, and with the support of my discernment team and my mentor, I was ordained a Deacon of the Ecumenical Catholic Communion on April . The processional hymn was "All Are Welcome," a statement of the inclu iv tyof God and of on Chn ch. When ask d t   he Bish-op' Who is calling or the ordination of Rosean Amaral as a deacon?," the memb rs of mye ntire commni tys tood pa   nd answered lodl y," We call for the ordination of Rosean Ama-ral!" I was b ingc alled ag in,f or the third time,a nd I ke w this was the ui ce of the bdyof   Christ.I answered,f rom the hyn n, "Here I am,L ord. I will hold yn   p op e in myhe art."

A WOMAN CALLED FATHER

Teri Harroun

I was not the little girl who dreamed of being a priest. I did not play church; I played school. I did not build an altar in my bedroom where I could pretend to preside; I built a hospital bed and with my med doctor bag attended to doll and stuffed animal patients. I would have told you that I loved everything about being Catholic, and in particular about Catholic school. I even loved the plaid skirts. I especially loved the plaid skirts.

I was not the little girl who dreamed of being a priest, but eventually I was the adult woman who heard a call that she could not ignore: the call to the vocation of priesthood.

For years before that, in spiritual direction, I kept telling my spiritual director that I felt God was grooming me for something but I did not know what it was. I was drawn to creating liturgy, and working in sacramental education. I was writing prayers and blessings that were being included in our church bulletin. As a member of a women's group that met every Monday evening

I was exploring the feminist contribution to Church, and I was inspired as well as challenged.

But I could not see what God was grooming me for.

As I passed my thirtieth birthday, and my third child was born, I started getting sick. A mystery kind of sickness. I was generally lethargic, and struggled to get every thing done. I was a stay at-home Mom, and I put the energy I had into my children and ignored my own needs. Sometimes I slept in my sweats, to save time getting myself dressed in the morning. My hair was falling out. My finger nails were breaking.

Then I started to feel nauseous, and had other digestive issues that could not be ignored. I ached everywhere in my own where I could quickly stop even with my three children in tow, to use the bathroom. Whatever was wrong with me was now evident to everyone in my family. So I started going to my doctor. We tried one diet change after another, letting at least six weeks pass before looking for the next thing. I went through many tests, and a few specialists. Eventually, after an endoscopy and biopsies it was determined that I had Celiac disease. The good news was that I now had a diagnosis and I did not have to take any medicine. But it also meant that I would have to commit to a new diet: gluten-free. I had no idea what that meant, but I committed one hundred percent on the day of my diagnosis. I did not even go home and have one last gluten meal. I never knowingly ate gluten (wheat, rye, barley, or oats) again. Within two weeks I felt better. Within a year, I felt like I had recovered.

I was diagnosed on a Wednesday. Going home I had lots of literature, and I started reading and researching. I focused on what I could eat, not what I now couldn't eat, and I joined a support group. One Saturday I went to church. I hadn't really thought ahead to what would happen during Mass. But as we got into the Eucharistic prayer it suddenly occurred to me, that I could not have Communion. I had been so immersed in my head and learning about Celiac disease, that I had neglected this detail: I could not receive Communion. I sat in the pew and my children and their father and the other people in our pew stepped over me on their way to Communion. My spirit was devastated. The words, "Lord, I am not worthy to receive you, but only say the words and I will be healed" bellowed in my head over and over, and I couldn't make the words stop. I am not worthy. I was not worthy. I could not receive. God was not healing me. And people I loved had stepped over me because they were worthy. I was not worthy.

Over time my Roman Catholic church worked with me. The low-gluten host that is offered still seemed to make me sick. But I could have wine if no one else drank from it. The wine itself was gluten-free, but the people who drank from that cup were not. So a separate chalice was put on the altar for me, and eventually I would share with another young girl who also had Celiac disease.

I thought about leaving Roman Catholicism at this point, and finding a denomination that offered true gluten-free hosts. But I also felt that this Catholic experience of God was pulling on my veins. I craved the smells and bells of Catholicism. And my particular faith community was very caring and empathetic. I knew that we the people were the Body of Christ, and I was receiving the full Communion of Christ through these people. As I told my spiritual director, "I am not having a crisis of faith; I am having a crisis of church!" And by "church" I meant the denomination. I chose to stay with my Roman Catholic Community.

But I could not see what God was grooming me for.

About a year later, many members of my Roman Catholic faith community decided to join the Ecumenical Catholic Communion (ECC). I was inspired to make this transition with them.

I had not experienced Catholicism so I genuinely committed to inclusion as what we found in the ECC. The ECC was an experience of Catholicism that I had not even dared to dream of. I was excited, and not the least bit tepid, about this new stained-glass shattering experience of God in a Catholic framework.

I was not able to attend our group's first Mass with an ECC priest, but the next week was there. This Mass was presided over by Fr. Scott Jenkins. I called him during the week to ask what I should do, since I couldn't receive Communion bread like everyone else. He was confused. I kept pursuing, figuring I would explain the separate chalice of wine solution that we had been using for a while. Finally he understood what I thought was my dilemma and said that there would be gluten-free hosts as well, and I could have one of those. We had this conversation on a Wednesday. Mass would be on Saturday.

Unlike when I was diagnosed with Celiac disease and did not spend time from Wednesday to Saturday contemplating the implications of Communion for me, from this Wednesday through Saturday all I could think about was Communion. Gluten-free Communion. I would be receiving Bread. The Body of Christ. Gluten-free. For me.

I should have worn a white dress. I should have worn a veil. I should have gone all out, because this celebration of Communion for me was as potent as the celebration of my First Holy Communion. I went to the back of the line, and processed forward. Everyone there knew my story, and as I approached, people in the pews were crying. I was crying. Fr. Scott was crying. Jesus had made this possible for me. Again, I had not even dreamed such a possibility for me. I was able to receive the Body of Christ. I was worthy.

Within weeks of being part of the Ecumenical Catholic Communion, people began to ask me about ordination. Was I considering priesthood? Didn't I feel called to the priesthood?

I had to ask Is p iesthood what God has b en g oomingm e for?

I colι d see the p eces of the p zle falling nto p ace. All ex ep one p ece. I hae Celiac disease and I cannot consm e g tι en. Translation: I cannot eat wheat. I cannot eat it. I am so sensitie that I hae p ob ems if I tou h it. Therefore,I cannot b eakb ead. I cannot sere b ead. How colι d God ps sib yb callingm e to the p iesthood? Yes,t here were g tι en-free hosts ax ilab e,b t most p op e receie d b ead that contained g tι en.

I talk d to bt h mys p ritα l director and myι car and shared that I thobι t I had a call to p iesthood. Btι the g tι en issu con- fonde d me. The fact that I was a woman did not enter into my hesitancy.B tι g tι ent— hat confonde d me.I was cons eled to write abtι Eu harist and Commni on ee ryda y. Theye ncon - ag d me to praya nd to write. So I did.I wrote abtι myF irst Commni on,w hich I rememb r iν iν dly.I wrote abtι b ingle - nied Communion, and my reflections of the Last Supper. I look d at the Tab e,e e n gi ng o chn ch ym yself one ee ninga nd sittingnde r the Altar as if it was a tent. I wrote abtι the linens, and the women who wash and iron the linens,a nd the b ead b k- ers and honey. I wrote abtι e ssels donated to the chn ch after trip to the HolyL and and the Tab rnacle. I wrote abtι candles and p ocessions and look ng nto someone's ey s as I sere Com- mni on.I wrote abtι intimacya nd hng r.I wrote and I wrote and I wrote.

After a few months,I ask d when wolι d I b done writing Mys p ritα l director and myι car bt h p oclaimed that they didn't kow . Theys eemed to thinkt hat I wolι d kow .

So I wrote some more.I wrote and I wrote and I wrote. And then one day,I realized: Commni on is alway p rt of the an- swer. Commni on is nee r p rt of the p ob em. In that moment I nde rstood,w holly,t hat I did not need to nde rstand. I did not need to kow whyG od wolι d call me to the p iesthood,b I did know that my call to preside at and serve Communion could not be the problem.

After that, to seminary I would go. The day I arrived at Iliff School of Theology in Denver, Colorado to begin classes for my Master of Divinity, I called my car from that parking lot, crying with joy, knowing that I was standing at the brink of my own life. It was a feeling of potential that I would never forget.

I was now the fully grown adult woman dreaming of priesthood, Catholic priesthood. God was grooming me. God is grooming me.

I was ordained a deacon on September 8th and a priest on September 22. The question I get asked most is "Why Father?" And my answer is quite lengthy. I had to pray and to pay to get to this naming for myself. I am glad for it to be a conversation starter: a conversation about not only how do we name ourselves, or our priesthood, but how do we name our image of God.

I have always been fascinated by women who wear men's clothes to do something that has traditionally been reserved for men: Joan of Arc, Thecla, Marian, Matilda of Tuscany, St. Pelagia, Marina the Monk, and (probably fictional) Pope Joan. Now, I am a woman, who is a mother, who people call Father, who wears what are traditionally men's clothes to do a job that has traditionally been reserved for men only, and those clothes happen to be dresses and robes and the job centers on serving food at a table. Clearly, God has a wonderful sense of humor.

It really started with my children, though. I have three children: Samantha, Nikolai, and Holly. I am very close to my kids. In the month before my ordination to the priesthood, my kids came to me and said, "Mom. We support your call to the priesthood. We believe you are a priest. We believe in your ministry, and we support you. But Mom, we want to be the only people who call you Mother."

Agreed.

But I turned the question back on them and said," Well, what should people call me for a title?"

They spent time on the question and came back to me and said," Father." Their reasoning was that the only way people would know that I was a priest, was to use the title Father, and they felt it was important that people know that I am a priest: a Catholic priest, called by God, supported by my faith community, and my children (and now my partner Bob who I hadn't even met at the time).

In their experience, when I was a student pastor at a Methodist community, I was called Reverend. Before I was ordained, people willingly and easily called me Reverend. And after my ordination, my children felt that my title should signify that call to which I was ordained, and the only word that made sense to them was Father.

They also enjoy telling people that their Father is also their Mother.

For me, I don't think all the female priests should use this title. It seems appropriate for me, at this time. It means something deeply to me, and the ministry that I am living into, and not just because of my children's request of me.

For instance, there are some who say that I can't have this role at all; that I cannot be an ordained Catholic female priest. And part of how that human notion got imposed on the Catholic psyche— that only men can be priests is— is that the role of priesthood was encapsulated in masculine language, and in particular the title of Father. And so, I claim it all. I claim the role, and I claim the name and title connected to that role.

Isn't it interesting that when I was a deacon people called me Deacon Teri. All masculine in language. Nobody ever suggested calling me Deaconess Teri. And when I was ordained into the priesthood, I was ordained a priest. Again, masculine language. Nobody suggested I be ordained a priestess. But when I claimed the masculine title of Father Teri, then people asked questions. Could that be because the most common name for God in our religious history is also Father, and we as a people of God in general have struggled to see the image of God in women? (Certainly not you nor I) But in our religious past of years of history, women have struggled to see the image of God in themselves. And that struggle was magnified by our general name of God as Father, and the men who stood as priest at altar and the women who were denied their call to stand as priest at altar.

I often have women tell me, after seeing me preside for the first time, the huge shift they see in themselves as they begin

I often have women tell me, after seeing me preside for the first time, the huge shift they see in themselves as they begin to glimpse the Divine that lies in them by seeing a woman as priest at table. So, on behalf of all women, not only those who are called to the diaconate or the priesthood, but all women, all women created in the love and image of God, the God who has most often been called Father, I claim the name of Father Teri.

Likewise, there are people who say the ECC is not Catholic. That we cannot claim the name Catholic with a big "C." They will tell us that we are heretics, schismatics, or some kind of Protestants. But we name ourselves. And we have named ourselves Catholic. With a big "C." So, what does that name mean to us? What does it mean to who we are? To who we are becoming? To our experience of God?

We are each baptized in Christ as priest, prophet, and king leader. How do we each live in that image? And what is our name? We ask our Confirmation youth this question, but as we grow I think we should continually ask ngon selves: What is our name in God?

There is a wonderful documentary called "I am Malcolm" about a UCC minister who is also post-surgery transgender male. He talks about himself and refers to Genesis 1:2v where it says, "So God created humanity in God's own image, in the image of God were they created; male and female God created them." And Malcom says that transgender individuals live this Scripture verse most fully, and are uniquely connected to God. But I think we all are made in God's image and we all have the potential to be the best of what is masculine while being the best of what is feminine, and I think in my case I want to name that and strive to live into that beautiful image of God both h/and in which I was created.

And while being a mother is the most profound experience of God that I have had, I also know that not all women are called to be mothers. Not all women are mothering persons. For those of us who are mothers, that is not the totality of who we are. By choosing the name of Father, I want us to remember that there are many ways that women contribute to church and to building God's reign in our world. For some of us, that way is mothering. But for many it is not. Think of Mary of Magdala, who was not a mother according to our Scripture, but a disciple of Jesus. But, over time, because she didn't connect to the acceptable archetype of mother in our church world, she was relegated to the alternative church archetype for women: seductress. It is only in modern times that she is redeemed, neither mother nor seductress but disciple, apostle, teacher, and leader.

I wonder what Mary of Magdala named herself.

Yes, I want us as the ECC to value mothering. And fathering. And sistering. And brothering. And friending. And stranger-ing. And discipling. And all loving.

Our faith community needs Mary of Magdala as much as we need Peter. We need a witness to the transfiguration and a witness to the resurrection. And both of these witnesses live in us. Again, the b st of what is feminine and the b st of what is mascu ine. In each of u . In on faith. In on tradition.

God is g ooming . We are worthy.

~

I hav also alway b en a pe t. I b liev Jesu was a pe t, and the Gosp l writer of John was a pe t and shows u the pe t side of Jesu . tiAfter b ingor dained, a lot of mype trye b ored myne w uc aon. Ev ntu lly had a bok þ ished called "A Woman Called Father: Reflections of Priesthood in a Woman's Body . The first poem is called "I am a Priest in Menopause", which reallys ets the theme of the whole bok . Here, I 'd lik to share another pe m from that bokw ith yu' This Hap ned."

This Happened

so
this.
"this hap ned"
as my Holly wou d say
y sterday, this hap ned

I had actu llydr eamed abu it b fore
worried abu it
wondered abu it
frank y, f eared it

in the instab lityof p ri-menop u e
which I ju t call menop u e
with its np edictab lity
nc ertainty

disreg rd for my ife or my s chedu e
y sterday,I gt my p riod
nkow n to me,of con se
I gt my p riod dn ingM ass
where I was the p iest and p esider
in my white rob
did I mention, white?
clothed in white
clothed in Christ
clothed in my B ap ismal gw n
clothed in my f ne ral p ll
clothed in Div nity
clothed in white
stained with b ood

it's the k nd of thing you don' t kow unless someone tells you
while ev ryne else kow s

I had actu lly dr eamed abu it b fore
worried abu it
wondered abu it
frank y,f eared it
and then, this hap ned

"oh well," was my first response
"I'm not su p ised"
"liv d throg t hat,di dn't I?"

why do I ev r worry

now today a s I p ay
I p ay w ith a new nde rstanding of God
of God,i n whose imag I am made
of God,w ho embdi es a woman's bdy
they ne v r teach yu hat!
of God,w ho b rths,a nd therefore
of God,w ho b eeds
of God,w ho b eeds not b cas e She is ctu or wonde d

of God,w ho b eeds b can e She has the pt ential to b rth
of God,w ho b eeds to cleanse
of God,w ho b eeds to refresh
of God,w ho b eeds ne p   ctedly
of God,w ho is not stained in b ood,b   anointed
of God,w ho b eeds b   mab   doesn't kow nl ess we tell Her;
shou d someone tell Her?
of God,w ho b eeds after b rthing
of God,w ho b eeds as I b eed
of God,w ho look forward to the p omise of not b eeding ny-
more
of God,w ho nn tn es others who b eed
of God,i n whose imag I am made
of God,i n whose imag I am made

this hap   ned.

"A Woman Called Father: Reflections of Priesthood in a Woman's Body"; Harron,F ather Teri; Fiv Oak Press; Pag 5

I AM SIX

Ann Poelking Klonowski

I am six

I was at Eileen's house, playing church. She was a nun with an apron for a veil, as was I. At the dressing table altar stood Timmy. He was the priest. We knelt before him.

"Why is *he* the priest?" I complained. "He is only five and we are seven. That's not fair."

"But he's the boy."

And that was the end of that discussion.

Sister asked how many sacraments there are and Mary Rose answered, "Seven for boys and six for girls."

And that was the end of that discussion.

I am seven.

I know the proper names for everything liturgical. Holy Communion was a "host," not a wafer, which is what the nuns at the hospital called it when she asked if I wanted communion on the night before my tonsillectomy. She used the wrong word. She was probably a Protestant trying to kill me by offering me food when I knew I was not allowed to eat anything. No fool I.

I knew all the names of the sacred vessels and which was which. I knew you had to be really, really holy to touch them, and only the anointed, sacred hands of the priest could touch the host. How I longed to be one of the boys who held the paten under the chins of communicants so not one sacred crumb would fall to the floor. If one did, there was a special sink in the sacristy to wash it down so it would go into a holy cistern, not the sewer. (I only knew this because my mother told me. I was not allowed in the sacristy.)

I wanted to be an altar boy so bad. I wanted to kneel on those hard, marble steps and say all those prayers with the priest. I already knew all the Latin, so why not? But, my mother reminded me, they were altar *boys*, not altar girls.

And that was the end of that discussion.

Not only did I know all the Latin, I knew what a chasuble was, as well as the maniple, the alb and cincture. I knew the liturgical colors and their significance. (I guiltily hoped someone would die so I could see the black vestments and complete my "pentafecta" of liturgical colors.)

Like all the little girls who still fit in their First Communion dresses, I was invited to participate in the Forty Hours procession. Before taking my place in the pew, I knew to genuflect on *both* knees when the Blessed Sacrament was exposed high on the altar in the glorious, gold monstrance. I also knew the word monstrance and that when the priest processed around the church, the extra vestment he wore over his shoulders was a cope. But even though I was the liturgical whiz kid and had all this amazing knowledge, I was still a girl.

112

And that was the end of that discussion.

___

I am twelve.

I am the church kid. My family was a wonderful Catholic family. We went to mass every Sunday, all the holydays of obligation, and confession every month. During Holy Week not everyone could get to church. There were little kids at home keeping Mom busy, and Dad was at work. So, being a good Catholic girl and wanting to fully participate, I walked to church. Occasionally I would recite the rosary as I walked, but ithely judging my classmates and neighbors who were playing outside while I, the good Catholic girl, walked to church for Holy Week. Despite my "judginess," I did engage in the liturgies and was deeply moved by them. But could I be anymore than a pew sitter for these sacred days? I could not.

And that was the end of that discussion.

___

I am eighteen.

I am at college and I know everything about religion. I can answer all the questions my friends ask about God and Catholicism. They are in awe. I should facilitate a discussion group open in the dorm. I invite them to Mass with me. Deb says it's OK, but she suggests that the priest not keep waiting and wash the dishes on his own time.

The following year I take a reprieve from church. I am going through the motions without feeling that I am present. I still go to mass when I am home with my family and don't discuss my troubled spiritual life with them. I still believe in God, and still believe that Jesus is gooey, but I need some space. I know I will be back

I take a break from the discussion.

___

I am twenty eight.

I am in my living room responding to a questionnaire from the diocese. The bishops are writing a letter on women and want to know what people think. As I fill out the questionnaire, the questions are increasingly grating. They are condescending and infuriating. I find myself becoming angrier and angrier.

Why, I ask myself, are they writing a letter about women? They have to ask women about women because they don't know about women. The bishops' earlier letters had been about poverty and racism—social problems. Apparently, *women* are a social problem. How could women possibly have any place of importance in the church? Eventually the letter idea was abandoned.

And that was the end of that discussion.

A male friend, a priest who is now married, told me about his training and first experience preaching. Seminarians were not permitted to have contact with women. When they went home for vacation, they were not to have any contact with women, not even their sisters. Women were, at best, aliens from another planet, and at worst, demons out to take their souls.

In time, my friend was ordained. When it was time to celebrate his first mass at his first assignment, he stood at the pulpit and froze. He could not speak. The assembly was filled with devils. Most of the people looking at him were women! How could he possibly go on? To this day he can barely remember how he managed to deliver that sermon. As he put it, he was so traumatized by his experience that he has shady memories of it. Eventually he overcame his terror, left the priesthood, and married a real, live woman.

I am in my thirties.

I participated in church as deeply as a married woman could. My spouse and I were involved in a variety of marriage and family ministries. I directed a small guitar group for liturgy. I helped with vacation Bible school. Although this was all important work, those were the only options open to me. What else could a woman do?

And that was the end of that discu sion.

I did hav one awesome voc ation.I was a mother,a holy call-ing This was a sp cial g ft reserv d only f or women. Who cou d ask f or any hing m ore?

Raising ds tak s a lot of time and attention. A mother can g t b y.B ut those k ds g ew and didn't need me at their elbw s ev ry m intu e.S o I went b ck o school.I thogt I wou d g t my teaching certificate back, but when I talked to the admissions cons elor, she ask d me, "If you cou d stdy any hing you d lik , what wou d it b ?"

"Theolog ," I rep ied.

"Then don't fool arond s cramb ing f or hon s with Eng ish and social stdi es.G et a master's in theolog .D o what you lov !"

I cou d not imag ne anyne p y ng m e to teach theolog ,b theydi d.F or six een y ars.

Until theydi dn't.

The daym yc ontract was not renewed was the most tram atic day of my life. I finally had the job I'd always wanted and it was tak n away f rom me b cau e I was foolish enogh t o stand p t a diocesan theolog eachers' in-serv ce to defend LGBT k ds. I had work d so hard for so long f or this job nd now it was all gne .G one.I was b ok n-hearted.

෴

My s p e challeng d me." What will hold you b cknow ?"

"Hold me b ck f rom what?"

"From ordination. You c ou dn't do it while you w ere work ng in a Catholic school,b what will hold you b cknow ?"

He reminded me of ev nts that I had allowed to p ss by ith little notice. As a memb r of ou Christian Life Commu ty,I freq ntly l ed on day long etreats. As a m ician,I had b en an integral part of planning and participating in a variety of litur-gies. I had often been asked to lead prayer services in a variety of circumstances. Future Church, a local progressive Catholic organization, asked me to preside at a program celebrating Mary of Magdala.

The kicker was when my spouse's cousins called and asked me to preside at their mother's funeral. They were not Catholic. They were members of a very small, very conservative church in the hills of southern Ohio. Their mother and father had helped found three churches in that area, yet their kids asked me to preside. So I did. I did it with ease and joy. The only one more surprised than my spouse was me.

At lunch after the funeral, I asked them why they invited me to preside.

"We thought you'd be good at it."

"But why did you think I'd be good at it?"

"Don't you do this at your school all the time?"

"No. I've never done anything like this in my life."

"Really? Well, we thought you'd do a good job. And we were right."

For the first time, this was not the end of the discussion.

My spouse was invited to an ordination of a woman in Chicago. He has no recollection of where the invitation came from, but he was intrigued and he went. He came home so thrilled by the experience that he went on about it at some length and with great fervor.

"You should go to the next one," he enthused. "You have to meet these women. I think you'll like them. You can check them out and see if they're people you'd like to be with."

I did go to the next one. And I did check them out and I did like to be with them.

I asked how to begin the process of preparation for ordination as a Roman Catholic woman priest. What a bizarre concept, I thought. And I don't even have to be a boy.

The discussion was taking an interesting turn.

There was so much to do before being accepted into the formation program. I wrote to the churches where I had been baptized, received first communion, confirmed, and married. I chuckled at the idea of the little old church ladies digging through files to find my sacramental history so that I could *make* sacramental history.

I acquired a spiritual director. I warned her why I needed to meet with her, that I was pursuing ordination as a priest. She could not have been more delighted! I took a battery of psychological tests and met with a psychologist three times so that she could pronounce me sane enough to get through the process, but, by definition, a little nuts to do so.

I had to convince my pastor to sign off on my character as a Catholic in good standing (which would not be the case when this was all over, so it seemed a bit hilarious). He was flummoxed by my wanting to be ordained to serve a church that didn't want me. When I asked him to be my liturgical mentor, he replied, "You have been here for twenty-five years. If you don't know how to preside at a liturgy by now, you weren't paying attention."

Later when I asked if he had a Vatican II sacramentary I could borrow, his answer was just as inviting "If you can't compose your own prayers, you have no business being a priest." Warm and fuzzy he is not. But despite his crankiness, he was a valuable mentor.

Getting into the work of the formal program took some doing. A life-long and very accomplished procrastinator, I could not get going. I analyzed and re-analyzed every bit of the instructions and every word I put on paper, mostly to convince myself that this was a terrible idea. There would be little flurries of activity. I would burst into enthusiastic paragraphs, only to stumble to a stop and begin to question everything I'd written, all that I had done to get here, every step along the way. After all the foot dragging, I found myself at the point in the process where I would be brought forward to be ordained a deacon. Why was I not more excited? What was wrong with me? Wasn't this something I had longed for since I was a little girl? Probably not.

~

I sat out on the patio behind the house. I loved to spend my prayer time there on the swing. I found it helped me to swing and breathe, swing and breathe. It helped get me into a meditative mood. That day was particularly lovely. The sky was clear, the air warm and dry, and absolutely still. A perfect day.

But as I sat there, I slowed, then stopped the swing so that I could write. I wrote in my prayer journal about what a fraud I was. Who was I to think I could be a priest? What a ridiculous idea. I wasn't holy enough. I wasn't capable of all that is required of a priest. All those people who had encouraged me were just being nice. This wasn't for me. This was the stupidest idea I had ever had. On and on it went, self-flagellating to an amazing degree.

It seemed that the discussion was over.

I stopped writing. As I sat there in the silent, still afternoon, the swing moved. I heard a voice in my heart say so clearly, " I bow where I will. Get out of my way." To say I was astonished is an understatement. Here I was, my finding my business in my own backyard, and I got my own personal Epiphany and Pentecost rolled into one.

I have not had a single doubt about my priesthood since that moment.

And the discussion continued.

Beverly, another woman who lives just a few hours from my home, was being ordained a deacon. I traveled there to help

with the ms ic for the litn g .I was ex ited for her.D n ing he
ceremony I could feel the joy filling the room. This was the first
ordination I had b en to since myH olyS p rit moment on the
swing After the celeb ation,I ap oached the women in the lead-
ershipc ircle for on reg on of p iests. What woh d they hink f
I were ordained a deacon when Bew as ordained a p iest? They
thoht it was a g eat idea.B t I wasn't sn e how Bew oh d
react.I mag ne myde ligt when she respnde d with enths iasm.
"I coh dn't thinkof a more wonderfh thing "

And the discs sion continu d.

After that,t here was no holdingm e b ck coh d not com-
þ ete myf ormation ni ts ḭ ck ye noh.M yc one rsations with
mys p ritu l director b came more animated.I was on myw ay.
When it came time for Bev s p iestlyor dination,I was ordained
a deacon.I was thrilled to þ eces when friends came all the way
from home to b with and spr t me that day.E e n more thrill-
ingv as the p esence of mys ib ing who came from their homes
see ral hon s away.

One b other had had nothing o do with this adv ntn e of
mine.H e thoht I was on the wrongs ide of chn ch teachinga nd
on myw aydow n the road to p rdition. Yet here he was at myor -
dination.I said to him," I thoht yuw eren't pf or this." With
a b gs mile on his face,he reþ ied," I am now, Annie! I am now!"
And deliv red a rik rack nghg

Once mydi aconal ordination was b hind me,I tookof f at
a g eat rate of sp ed.I t tooka few v ryl ongm onths to reach
p iestlyor dination.I had one p ay r as the dayb g n: that I
coh d b totallyp esent to the ceremony. As I layp ostrate on
the floor, I heard and loved every saint in the litany, especially
myow n "small s" saints,m yb loe d familya nd friends. At the
lay ngon of hands ḭt he assemb y,I had seen other ordinands
p ay rfh lyc lose their ey s.B t when p oþ e came pt o lay

hands on me,s ome of them strang rs,s ome of them v ryde ar,
and esp ciallym ys ps e and children and g andchildren,a ll I
col d do was smile,s o g atefl for the b essing rainingdow n on
me. What a joy li ev nt!

Ev r since that day,I hav ex rcised myp iestlyoc ation þ
p esidinga t Mass,v siting he sickc onsoling he g iev ngv alk-
ingv ith the trob ed,a nd p esidinga t wedding and fne rals.
All of them in their own way are filled with joy. I cannot imagine
any hinga s wonderfl as this,p ay ngv ith the p oþ e of God,
serving them and their families, and helping them find their own
way.

I have had so much good in my life: a loving family, fulfill-
ingv orka nd god f riends. As x la b e as all these are and hav
b en,t here has b en nothing ik this ministry.I hav b en so
g atefl .I am so g atefl .I will continu to b g atefl .

And the discu sion continu s!

I'M GOING TO BE A PRIEST

Rosa M. Buffone

> "'Love the Lord your God with all your heart and
> with all your soul and with all your mind and with all
> your strength.' The second is this: 'Love your neighbor
> as yourself.' There is no commandment greater than
> these."
>
> Mark 12:30-31 New International Version (NIV)

Rosa!
I would hear my mother's voice ringing through the house or be carried by the wind around the neighborhood calling me to whatever needed attention at that moment. Visit Mrs. Fitchett. Feed the fish. Teach your sister. Give "them" yours. Be a good friend. Show kindness and understanding

God's voice was equally distinct in the echo of prayers and songs at Mass, the laughter around friends and family, the waves at the beach or the light of stars and moon at night. Visit the sick

Feed the hungry. Teach my word. Give to the poor. Befriend the lonely, lost, troubled. Be compassionate and loving

I was five years old playing with my cousins in the front yard at my grandparents' house. Everyone was coming for the outdoor house Mass with Don Enzo, great uncle Tony's brother visiting from Brazil.

"Rosa, come here, we're getting ready." I ran to join my parents and others gathered on the back yard patio. I sat on my dad's lap next to my mother on the cement wall around the perimeter while others sat on an assorted collection of chairs closer to the card table with a white table cloth making the altar. Don Enzo stood and Mass started with a hymn on the tape player, everyone still sitting, singing a long in Italian. It was hot and I fussed more than once, especially during the homily. But next was Communion, I loved when the bells rang at church and the priest held up the cup and the plate. I felt something special in my heart. I wondered if Don Enzo had a bell. A fancy glass and plate with grandpa's homemade wine and grandma's fresh baked bread was on the table. Uncle Tony went and stood next to his brother and while one held up the cup the other the plate. Don Enzo began his prayer in Italian, yet I was hearing in my heart, "this will be you one day." I knew it to be true. After Mass, my mother and I walked up to Don Enzo for a child's blessing. I love Don Enzo to this day. He was gentle and loving and doing God's work in the missions. Don Enzo smiled, and placing his hand on my head, consecrated me with the sign of the cross on my forehead and the words *"bellisima de Dio,"* not knowing then that this would be a precursor to my Ordination.

I remember telling my mother a few days later that I was going to be like Don Enzo, a priest! Only to hear through her chuckles, "...maybe a nun, but not a priest. Girls cannot be priests in the Church." I affirmed "yes I will," and ran off to play.

Since that day, my journey has taken many paths in answering the "call" to priesthood, just not in the Roman

Rosa M. Buffone

Catholic Churches— so in that respect, my mother was right. I've been a Girl Scout, babysitter, Eucharist Minister, Pastoral Council Member, facilitator of my RCC LGBTQ Adult Faith Sharing group and Adult Advisor to the closeted and questioning youth, Mental Health Counselor, Chaplain, friend, daughter, sister, niece, cousin.

I can't say my spiritual journey has been an intimate one with Jesus of Nazareth, but I've known his peace and light, inclusivity, healing truth, and shepherding way through the Cosmic Christ.

I've known God's call, presence, protection and unconditional love as a white, gay woman of peasant immigrant parents my entire life.

I've known the Holy Spirit's power to part the sea, guide the way and make all things possible.

I've known the Blessed Mary's tender touch, sacred heart, courageous strength and love beyond all pain.

In 2011 I attended the Ecumenical Catholic Communion retreat in Rochester, N.Y. It was an intimate gathering and Edwina Gateley was the keynote speaker. When she read, "God Knows. God Understands." from her poem *Let Your God Love You*, I knew all would be well. It was at that same retreat that I experienced my first Mass presided by a woman Catholic priest. My heart swelled, my words rambled as I described it all to my mother afterwards. Looking into each other's eyes, I paused and said, "I'm going to be like her. I'm going to be a priest." My mother affirmed, "I know you are." Ordination day, my mother blessed me from heaven and I knew her presence and love was enfolding me as I was vested in chasuble by my dad, my wife, my sister, relatives and friends.

At the time of this writing I am a Priest in the Ecumenical Catholic Communion and serving as Pastor to Holy Spirit Catholic Community. I know with God all things are possible. I will answer the call every day," Here I am Lord,I have heard you calling n the night ...I will g L ord,I will hold you p op e in myhe art."

FOUR POEMS and an ESSAY

"don't read the comment sections"

Teri Harron

I had to read the words twice
to really understand
when you called me
a sacrilegious charade
a scam
a revisionist
a narcissist
big as a Bull
a feminist fraud
the woman who,' latae sententia' ex ommni cated herself
passing herself off as a priest;
yes,twice I read it
all of it
to remember
you were talking about me
when what I wanted you to know
is that I am kind,
I wanted to be the kindest person you ever met
on a Tuesday
because I seem to be my best on Tuesday
but I read your words on Saturday
in the morning
and I didn't feel kind
I wanted to tell you
that when you call me those things
you call God those things
not because I am God
but because I am God's

as are you
so I will wait until Tuesday to tell you
you're right,
I am a revisionist.

© Teri Harron,

Praise Poem on the Occasion of Ordination
September 8, 2009

Sheila Dunken Dierks

Glory Be! You made us all,
each one ripened in the womb of a woman,
each of us, completely embraced for three full seasons,
each labored over, brought forth, held.
Out of/into love.
You wrap us in the swaddling linen of your delight and hope.
You raise us.
You know our own woman names, written on the palm
of Your divine hand before the dawn of time.
And now, our truth, our call, Your hope lies prone
As the cloud of witnesses are sung
All of holy women and men, pray for us.
We are, through Your imagination, brought to living
by a woman and now
You sacred forever wish unfolds
before an altar.
You entice us, womb deep being that we are
to embrace Your rejoice and labor for You
to write our sacred names on our palms
and speak You forth in joy.
Your will be done!

Forte Rapariga ,Forte Mulher*

Rosean Mae Amaral

I am a big woman
with legs like tree trunks
and arms like thick tree branches.
A strong woman.

I am firmly rooted
to the Feminine Earth Mother
though other forces sometimes cause me to bend
to the breaking point,
constantly trying

My soul is shared with all that has gone before,
all that is present,a nd all that is yet to come.
Therefore,I am not bound by the patriarchal beliefs and values
of this world.

I do not have "power over" anyone ,nor do I wish to.
But I do dream and long
To have "power with"
the all-encompassing wisdom
of existence.

I am a BIG woman.

*Portuguese for strong little girl,strong woman

The Darkness and the Dream
Kae Madden

I have been spinning for a long time, Lord.
You have given me
Cords of
despair to spin into joy,
confusion to spin into trust,
doubt to spin into faith,
selfishness to spin into Love.

I have spent many hours
Laboring to spin thread
Of gold and silver and bright colors
From happiness and pride.

I began a caterpillar,
I still am,
Slow and clumsy,
Inching an existence
In a world that was
Very small
And defined by what I could see
From my lowly
Vantage point.

I moved
From place to place
With one purpose —
Filling my hunger
From things of earth.

Called and Chosen

Gradually,
My physical hunger abated
And a calm winged emptiness
Overcame me.

I was drawn to You, Lord,
Though I knew You not,
Drawn to spin–
Through I knew not what or why.

Day by day,
You presented me
With threads of my humanity,
Challenging me
To spin Your ways
Around and through
Until the cord reflected You –
The thread of Humanity–
My thread –
Interwoven with Your Divinity.

Unknowingly,
I have enclosed myself –
With my spinning
Your spinning
I saw the last glimmer
Of the naked world
Yesterday.
The spinning must cease for now.

Now I am in total darkness
Surrounded by
Cords of many colors
That I cannot see,

Four Poems and an Essay

Hungering for
A release from inch-by inch
Existence.

Believing—
From a center I cannot tap
That You have a plan,
A secret,
That I must wait for,
In suspense.

I'll wait, Lord,
Though I am in darkness,
I wait.
It is quiet here
If I stop the chattering of my mind.
It is peaceful
If I call a truce with the warring of my soul.
I must rest
And wait…

Someone told me a story once
of a glorious creature
called a butterfly…
what a strange and glorious creature.

WHEN GRANDMOTHERS GET ORDAINED
Sheila Duncan Dierks

It is left to my grandmother-imagination, what experiences do young women have in Roman seminaries as they approach their diaconal ordinations? Do they design the invitations and have them printed? Do they, with their discernment committees, write the liturgy? Do they go to the bishop for a conversation about how the commitment vows will be phrased and who will be included in the Litany of the Saints? Do they have to make sure that everyone has hotel reservations and enough crib for grand-babies? Who makes up the beds? And what about dinners for all the nights that the family and friends will be in town hanging out on the back porch and in the family room? Who doesn't eat beef? Who is allergic to milk? And who checks to see that there is enough beef, food and wine? When those young women are ordained will they be surrounded in every place whom they know and love, in a church building that they know as home? And what about the prostration cloth?

These are the blessed events of ordinations that happen to those of us who have had to wait till later years, to those of us who are female. I am sixty five, called to ordination since the age of five. Now I am honored with a great family, grown children, a spouse husband and a number of grandchildren. None of this would be mine if I had been ordained in the early. None of this would have happened if it had not been for the open arms of the Ecumenical Catholic Communion. I have been embraced and raised up and discerned in a community. The discerning committee is full of people with whom I worship and eat pasta after Saturday afternoon Mass in a blessed extension of Eucharist. I am, as in the early church, scrutinized and affirmed by those with whom I celebrate every week. No strangers here.

In addition, there is the long journey of education and honing of academic and spiritual skills at Iliff School of Theology in Denver. That has been gi ng on f or better than two years. It continues for another academic quarter or two.

And so, on March 3B ishop Peter Hickman, pastor of St Matthew Church in Orange, C A and bishop of the Ecumenical Catholic Communion arrived and stayed at our house. He sat at the breakfast table with grandchildren and children, with bowls of cereal and cups of tea, the New York Times and Cheerios on the rug. He has small children of his own, so none of this is new.

The week before the ordination, I was the homilist and talked about the theology of touch. Samuel touches the head of David, Jesus touches the eyes of the man born blind. Sacred work. God present. For the last three years, the members of the community have touched me, literally sign of peace, gift of bread and wine. Jesus present in their touch. My theology assures me that the bishop comes to ordain with the laying on of hands and to affirm what the community has already done, already ordained. His presence, his sacramental touch, is a public acknowledgment of what is already being accomplished. We know this, it is affirmed in word when the community publicly, in one voice, calls me forth, and says they believe I am ready to be diakonos to them.

The sacred surprise of my parish, Light of Christ is that they, we, believe that we have the power of discernment and recognition and lifting of individuals to do and be in service to each other.

This is as human be and hopeful a community as I have had the pleasure to know. We believe that Jesus is present in not only the elements but truly and deeply in the members of the community. There is clearness and veracity and possibility in the midst of the humanness.

So what about that prostration cloth? Following the homily on the sacred nature of touch, we all, perhaps a hundred of us, went into the hall and dipped our hands in blue, yellow and green acrylic paint and laid our palm prints on the wheat-colored cotton length. When it dried it was sewed to be a prostration cloth, six feet long a nd three feet wide,ha nds i̇ sib e front and b ck. At the ordination,i t was danced in with on entrance p ocession and laid on the g ond i n the aisle for me to lie on while myC lod of Witnesses was sngo̱v   r ꜱ all. The theologꝗf Jesꜱ -spr   ted commɴi tyw as made i̇ sib e in ev̇ ryha nd p int. We do not wait on those from ot̄ side. We b liev̇ that the face, the v̇ ryp esence of the Christed one,i s in each of ꜱ ,a nd we all are the workof his hands.

Ordination within su h a Commɴi on is b essedlẏf l̇ l of the old-into-new. We are restoring̱ he most i̇ tal role of the indiv̇ d- a l hm an commɴi tẏi n oḇ eri̇ ngꝑ aẏ ngꝼ or,b liev̇ ng̱ n, g̱ i̇ ng̱g̱   dance and sending̱ꝼ orth. Theẏꜣow   me.I hav̇ some "warts" so theẏa re ini̇ ted to b critical and to act as edɑ ators. Theẏꜣop   with and for me. I will b no strang r to them as I serv̇ in their midst.

Perhaꝑ the nek̇ g eat son ce of vc ations is g andmothers. We ꜣow   well what it is to wash feet,a s well as hands,f aces and assorted bd ẏꝑ rts. We ꜣow   well what it is to p aẏw ith and for those arond ꜱ . We maẏb   well v̇ rsed in scriꝑ n e from v̱ ars with on Bib es. We hav̇ b en trained in ꝑ tience and hoꝑ -ag inst-hoꝑ ,i n forg̱ i̇ ng̱a nd startingꝺv̇ r. And we ꜣow   so well what it is to set the tab e,t o serv̇ on b st ꜣ nꝗ t meal, and to ini̇ te all to b welcome and all to share the feast.

REFERENCES

ABC/Snc oast." Sarasota woman say she's a Catholic p iest." March ,B

Catholic Chn ch of the Resn rection B *Vocation to the Priest-hood*,a ccessed after 1 1 B< http //wwwr esn rection. coz a/main/sacraments/7 2 >

de Waal, Esther. *Seeking God: The Way of St. Benedict.* Minnesota: The Litn g cal Press,0

Dierk ,S heila Dn k n. *WomenEucharist*.B ou der,C olorado: Woe nWord Press,9

Eisen,U te. *Women Officeholders in Early Christianity: Epigraphical and Literary Studies.* Minnesota: The Litn g cal Press,0

Green,G raham. *Twenty-one Stories*.L ondon: Peng n Book , 9

Harron, Teri. *A Woman Called Father: Reflections of Priesthood in a Woman's Body*.N ewb g,N Y: Fir Oak Press,0

Lei tt,J di th." Women as Priests." New York Times,S nda y Rei ew,S ep emb r 9B

Ly ns, Tom." Relig on Frad or Religion Coni ction." *Sarasota Herald Tribune*,F eB

Macy,G ary. *The Hidden History of Women's Ordination: Female Clergy in the Medieval West.* Ox ord: Ox ord Unir rsity Press,0

Meehan,B ridg t Mary.M aryM other of Jesn Incln ir Catholic Commni tyL itn g .J ne 9B <http //b idg tmary b og-

spt c om/ß   6 mary mother-of-jess -incls iv -catholic.
html>

Scott, Anna. *Sarasota Herald Tribune.* Feb6   h,0

Teresa of Av la. *Interior Castle.* London, Thomas Bak r,2

The Irish Life of Brigit cited in Oliv r Dav es,e d. *Celtic Spirituality.*N ew YorkP   ali ist,P ress, 9   .

DEACON ROSEAN MAE AMARAL—Rosean Mae Amaral completed four years of study in the program of Theological Education for Ministry, and was a Stephen Minister for 5 years. She was ordained as a deacon of the Ecumenical Catholic Communion in 0 She and Lannie, her partner of thirty one years, are the parents of four children who have blessed them with ten grandchildren.

REVEREND ROSA M. BUFFONE— Rosa M. Buffone was ordained to the diaconate in 20 and presbyterate in 00 She is a founding member and pastor of Holy Spirit Catholic Community and vicar of the ECC Northeast Region for three OPB terms. She is married to Sandy Rice, and a proud aunt, loving sister, and devoted daughter, niece, and cousin.

REVEREND SHEILA DURKIN DIERKS— Sheila Durkin Dierks experienced a persistent invitation to ordination beginning when she was called at age seven. Now married to Peter, mother to four, grandmother to eight, mentor to many, she was ordained a deacon in the Ecumenical Catholic Communion in 0 and a priest in 0S she loves her journey.

BISHOP DENISE DONATO—Denise Donato is the founder and pastor of Mary Magdalene Church in East Rochester, NY. She and her husband Phil recently celebrated 40 years of marriage. They have three grown children, four beloved grandchildren and are eagerly awaiting the birth of twins which will raise that number to six

REVEREND KATHLEEN GORMAN— Kathleen is blessed by her beloved partner, Tracy's love and companionship Kathleen loves baring witness to those she walk with in hosp ce and p lliativ care and in seriv ng the commni ty at Holy Family. For fn, Kathleen lov s to hik ,do y rdworka nd p ayou side!

FATHER TERI HARROUN— Fr. Teri is a gluten-free gummy-bear loving poet, partner, parent, and priest. She serves as pastor at Light of Christ in Longmont, Colorado and enjoys reading, crocheting, walking, and moose-ology (all the things you learn about God when you get yourself caught between a mama moose and her babies).

MARY E. HUNT, PhD .— Mary E. Hnt is a feminist theolog an who is co-fonde r and co-director of the Women's Alliance for Theolog , Ethics and Ritu l (WATER). A Catholic activ in the women-chn ch mov ment and on LGBTIQ matters, she lectn es and writes on theolog and ethics with particu ar attention to liberation issu s. She is an editor of *A Guide for Women in Religion: Making Your Way from A to Z* (Palg av , 9 9 and co-editor with Diann L. Neu of *New Feminist Christianity: Many Voices, Many Views* (Sk igt Paths,0 .

REVEREND ANN POELKING KLONOWSKI— Ann Klonowsk was ordained a p iest on Sep emb r 7 20 She earned a b chelor's deg ee in edu ation and a master's deg ee in relig on std - ies. She has b en a committed teacher, and has b en activ in her chn ch since her colleg day . She is the mother of two adu t children of whom she is ridicu os ly p od , and has two incredib y intellig nt g anddaht ers.

REVEREND KAE MADDEN—K ae Madden is p iv leg d to serv as Pastor, Chn ch of the Belov d, Northglenn CO since 9 . Kae lik s to create art with oil p stels, soak p Natn e and is fed y Centering Pray r and Tai Chi Chih. The story of her life in six words: *Crossroads, Invitation, Choose Life, Impossible Possible.*

Contributors

BISHOP BRIDGET MARY MEEHAN— Bridget Mary Meehan, MA, DMin, ARCWP, is the author of twenty books on prayer and spirituality. She presides at inclusive Catholic liturgies and weddings in Sarasota, Florida. She is a bishop serving the Association of Roman Catholic Women Priests, dean of Global Ministries University's Doctor of Ministry and Master of Divinity Programs, and co-founder of People's Catholic Seminary.

REVEREND MARY RAMERMAN— Rev. Mary Ramerman is a Catholic priest in Rochester, New York. Ordained in 2001 she is the founding pastor of Spiritus Christi and has served there for twenty years. Mary's courageous spirit and daring leadership have empowered her congregation to develop outreaches to the marginalized and to address global crises such as climate change and immigration.